New

Birds Worth Watching

Birds Worth Watching

by

George Miksch Sutton

Foreword by Olin Sewall Pettingill, Jr.

UNIVERSITY OF OKLAHOMA PRESS : NORMAN AND LONDON

Books by George Miksch Sutton:

Birds Worth Watching (Norman, 1986)
Bird Student: An Autobiography (Austin, 1980)
*To A Young Bird Artist: Letters from Louis Agassiz Fuertes to
   George Miksch Sutton* (Norman, 1979)
Fifty Common Birds of Oklahoma and the Southern Great Plains
   (Norman, 1977)
Portraits of Mexican Birds: Fifty Selected Paintings (Norman, 1975)
At a Bend in a Mexican River (New York, 1972)
High Arctic (New York, 1971)
*Oklahoma Birds: Their Ecology and Distribution, with Comments on
   the Avifauna of the Southern Great Plains* (Norman, 1967)
Iceland Summer: Adventures of a Bird Painter (Norman, 1961)
Mexican Birds: First Impressions (Norman, 1951)
Birds in the Wilderness (Norman, 1936)
Eskimo Year (New York, 1934; new edition, Norman, 1985)
The Exploration of Southampton Island, Hudson Bay (Pittsburgh, 1932)
An Introduction to the Birds of Pennsylvania (Harrisburg, 1928)

Library of Congress Cataloging-in-Publication Data

Sutton, George Miksch, 1898–1982
   Birds worth watching.

   Includes indexes.
   1. Birds—United States—Addresses, essays,
lectures. I. Title.
QL682.S87   1986   598.2973   86-1314
ISBN 0-8061-1975-6

Published 1986 by the University of Oklahoma Press, Publishing Divi-
sion of the University, Norman. All rights reserved. No part of this book
can be used without written permission of the publisher. First edition.
Printed in Japan.

Contents

Foreword

Whenever I was afield with George Sutton during our days together in graduate school at Cornell University and in many of the years to follow, it seemed that nothing ever missed his discerning eye. His perceptions were infectious, sharpening my own senses. In this very same way he affected his many students at the University of Oklahoma from the time he joined its faculty in 1952.

Birds Worth Watching reflects George Sutton, the consummate field man. The sixty species he chose for this book are well known, some distributed widely, others restricted to particular places. Although he occasionally included some of his observations of them in Iceland, the Far North, and Mexico, his accounts pertain primarily to birds in the forty-eight contiguous states and, not unexpectedly, very often birds in Oklahoma.

Throughout the accounts George Sutton's legendary flair for enjoyable writing is at its best, replete with charming insights on different species drawn from his intimate familiarity with them.

This book might well have been titled "Birds Worth Knowing About," since the recurring feature in all the accounts, which was the author's basic motive in writing them, is the pinpointing of what we still need to learn about even our most common species. He raises questions about the functions of certain of their physical peculiarities and behavioral traits that have always puzzled him and about which answers are still lacking. Nobody will read this book without acquiring incentives for watching and studying all of the sixty species more closely.

Olin Sewall Pettingill, Jr.

Preface

When I was very young I loved birds dearly, but I don't remember being puzzled by them. The handsome Ruffed
Grouse that came to our cabin in the woods near Aitkin,
Minnesota, to drum every day on the sill of the big window
in the living room came because it had found that sill a
good place for drumming. Grouse the world over had their
favorite windowsills and that was where they drummed.
Why they drummed didn't bother me in the least. Why they
were the only birds of our neighborhood that drummed
didn't bother me. I watched and listened enchanted, slowly
coming to realize that "our bird" had some sort of schedule. It came about breakfast time, and if I watched closely I
would see it walking slowly back and forth with head low
and wings pressed tight against its body; then, impelled
by the urge to perform, it would fluff its plumage, lift its
head high, spread and lower its wonderful fan of a tail,
hold its chest close to the glass, and thump its sides with
wings that moved so swiftly I could hardly see them. Sometimes the feathers of that chest actually touched the glass.

The drumming started with two muffled thumps, a full
second or so apart, followed by a whir that was spellbinding. So powerful were the strokes of those two wings that
the whole bird was lifted and spun around a little by them.
I wondered why all that beating didn't carry the bird off,
but there it stayed. And there it drummed over and over
until, satisfied that it had made itself heard, it flew off.

The year was 1901. I was three years old. I didn't even
know that drummer of ours was a male bird. Its drumming
entertained me in a way that I find impossible to describe.
Every blessed thing it did on that windowsill gave me a

feeling approaching ecstasy. But I was not puzzled. Grouse drummed. It was their way. What I was seeing time after time told me precisely what they did while drumming, but I wasn't puzzled by any of it.

When the Sutton family moved back to Bethany, Nebraska, where my father was a professor of elocution at the now defunct Cotner College, I would see no Ruffed Grouse anywhere, but I was too young, too inexperienced, to wonder why. The word "habitat" wasn't in my vocabulary. The birds that demanded my attention were the Blue Jays that nested in a boxelder tree near the house; the Barn-Owls that lived in the college tower; the Bee Martins (Eastern Kingbirds) that I saw and heard every day, and the meadowlarks that were singing everywhere. I didn't know the meadowlarks were Western Meadowlarks. I knew just that they were meadowlarks and that their song whipped out the words "I'll steal your wheat, young man!" And there were those sparrow-sized birds that people called "Dickchisels" that sang their monotonous, four-syllabled song in every alfalfa field.

All of these birds interested me. I never tired of watching and listening to them. But they did not puzzle me.

Then, little by little, I began to realize that the small, black-looking, wide-winged birds that the neighbors all called Chimney Swallows *did* puzzle me. Why did I never see one of them alight anywhere? Didn't they have feet? Always, always, always, they were in the air circling about endlessly, chasing each other as if playing some game, never resting. Now and then I'd see one drop into a chimney and I'd wonder what it could be doing down there in the dark. Never having handled one, I had no idea how powerful its sharply clawed toes were. How in the world could any bird cling to a vertical brick wall? As for the species' nesting habits, I was completely bewildered. No book that I had told me of the neat little basket of twigs that the birds glued to the bricks with their own saliva. I was truly, and deeply, puzzled. Had I known that the great Greek savant Aristotle, who worked out a classification of birds three centuries before Christ, had called that little bird's Old World relatives the Apodi, the Footless Ones, I might have been comforted.

I'm still puzzled by some things that Chimney Swifts do. I know that they gather twigs for the nest while flying, clutching them in their feet and breaking them from a dead branch, but I don't know when they coat them with that viscous saliva of theirs. Do they give them the saliva treatment as they fly to the home chimney, or do they wait until they are clinging to the bricks at the nest-site proper? And do they ever—*ever* is a strong word—snatch a dead twig from the ground or pull it free from an old nest?

Birds that also puzzled me were the "Bullbats," whose correct name was Common Nighthawk. These had a way of plunging from the sky straight toward the ground, winding up the swift descent with a roar or boom that was almost frightening. How did the birds make it? Was it vocal or did air rushing through or past the stiffly held, long wing feathers produce the awesome sound? The birds never boomed over our house, though one of them often spent the day, apparently asleep, perched lengthwise on the ridgepole of our woodshed.

Then came my first bird book, Frank M. Chapman's *Bird-Life*, with its colored pictures by Ernest Thompson Seton. Those beloved parents of mine, wondering what to do with a son who obviously doted on birds and didn't seem to be interested in anything else, had ordered it for me. It became a focal point of my life, gave direction to my every thought and move. Never did I read it from cover to cover. Indeed, I read in it very little; but I looked at the color-plates over and over, often wondering why I had failed to see so many of the species pictured. I did not realize that the book was really about eastern, not midwestern, birds. The meadowlark that it described so well was the Eastern Meadowlark. The meadowlark that I was hearing every day was the Western Meadowlark. I didn't know it at the time, but the songs of the two species differed greatly.

I especially enjoyed the picture, opposite page 90, of a

Chimney Swift clinging to its strange, fragile-looking bracket of a nest inside a chimney. So all those black-looking "swallows" that kept circling around were not swallows after all. They were swifts. They were not, in other words, closely related to the swallows that nested every summer in the big Aspinwall barn. It was great fun expounding to the neighbors about these swifts, whose nests I wanted so much to see. Alas, no one encouraged me to climb about on the rooftops in hopes of looking down into chimneys. "What are you going to do with that boy?" I could hear the neighbors asking my parents. "He'll break his neck."

Grant Aspinwall, a lad of my own age who lived across the creek from our house, was a fellow bird student. It was he who found the dead Bee Martin in the road, who helped me wash the mud from its plumage and swing it back and forth in the sun and wind until it was dry. It was he who followed with me the shy little bird that sang *wichery, wichery, wichery* in the tall weeds along the creek. That little bird was the Maryland Yellow-throat, pictured opposite page 162. And it was Grant who, having killed one of the Aspinwall chickens, cut it up with me in our cool "laboratory" under the bridge, learning there how the gizzard and liver and intestines were all hung together in one glorious *tout ensemble*.

The birds that puzzled me most were, I believe, the blackbirds, great numbers of which passed over our house every day in late summer and fall. Where they came from and where they were going was a mystery. There must have been hundreds of thousands of them. I didn't know what they were, though I could tell that they were black or at least very dark. They probably were Common Grackles, Brown-headed Cowbirds, and Red-winged Blackbirds on their way to a communal roost, but I never found the roost.

George Miksch Sutton

Acknowledgments

The University of Oklahoma Press gratefully acknowledges the aid of John S. Shackford, who helped seek out and assemble the uniquely appropriate photographs used in this book. We also acknowledge the contributions of Gary D. Schnell, Jack D. Tyler, and William A. Carter, who helped edit the manuscript, and Sonya E. Johnson, who typed many drafts as the book took shape. No doubt the author would have thanked many others for their help in preparing the book. The Press regrets that their names are not available for recognition here.

Publication of *Birds Worth Watching* has been aided by a grant from the Oklahoma Ornithological Society.

Bird Accounts

Common Loon

(Gavia immer)

He who has never heard a Common Loon has yet to hear one of Nature's most beautiful sounds. Even memory of that high, clear "holler," drifting down from the sky or through mist from a far corner of the lake, sets my spine to tingling.

On May 12, 1926, a Common Loon in breeding feather was brought alive to my office in Harrisburg, Pennsylvania. The big bird probably had mistaken a wet road for a stream, had crash-landed there, and, unable to take off without a stretch of open water in which to work up speed, had submitted to capture.

From tip of bill to tip of outstretched feet (not of stubby tail) that loon was just over three feet long and weighed almost eight and a half pounds. Its heaviness was, I knew, partly because none of its bones were hollow, a condition that reduced buoyancy, hence helped with fishing well below the water's surface. The black of the bird's head and neck plumage had a faint green and purple shine, while that of its back, though less iridescent, was spangled with pure white spots that reminded me of a layout for the tents of an army's bivouac. Its eyes were a deep shade of red.

The loon had been captured not far from Philadelphia. It refused fish that we brought for it, but seemed not to be injured, so we decided to affix an official leg-band and release it at the lake in Wildwood Park. What I recall most vividly about it as it quieted down in my arms was its deep, slow breathing. I couldn't feel its heart beat but, as its plumage shifted with expansion and contraction of its rib-cage, I could not help wondering how long it could hold its breath, whether normal apnoea would allow it to pursue

3

prey at a considerable depth, and whether oxygen stored in muscles would be depended upon in routine capture of food. What a marvelous armful that bird was!

Freed at the water's edge, the loon swam off sedately, dipped its bill in the water several times, and went under when about fifty yards from shore. Not for a long time did we see it again. When it did show up, it was in the very middle of the lake. No one could find it on the lake the following day, but a loon seen on the Susquehanna River may well have been the same bird. Over a year later (on May 31, 1927) I received word that remains of "my" banded loon had been found near the town of Brighton, on the north shore of Lake Ontario, by a man who believed it had been "killed by a skunk, as the approach and attack were all clearly indicated in the sand."

Strictly a bird of the Northern Hemisphere (few, if any, records are from south of the equator), *Gavia immer* is strongly migratory, for it depends on open water for its food. Adult birds lose their bright plumage in the fall, becoming plain gray above and white below. This dull plumage is what most birds that we see in the southern Great Plains are wearing in October and November, but some are in bright plumage and we cannot avoid suspecting that adult birds lose their body feathers at differing times, some slightly later than others, while gray birds are adults that have completed the molt and young of the season in their first winter feather.

Eager to learn all that was known, I wrote Judith W. McIntyre, a recognized authority on loons, asking her to tell me what she had ascertained about the Common Loon's molts. She replied that such numbers of loons molt their body plumage before migrating southward from the breeding ground that parts of Lake Michigan are "floating with feathers" in the fall; that these same birds "lose their wing quills later, on the wintering ground"; that immature birds two or three months old achieve a juvenile plumage that is kept through fall and winter; and that these young birds

Common Loon, *Gavia immer*. Alaska, 1980. © Jim Zipp/National Audubon Society Collection, PR.

have a complete molt that makes them flightless for some time in May, June, or July. She stated further that breeding adults begin to molt around the bill, some having a "white beard" for a time, then a nearly white face. In her winter fieldwork along the coast of Virginia she "noted flightless birds from the end of January through early March."

How old were these flightless birds? Might some have been immature, molting a bit earlier than most birds of that age group usually do? Questions of this sort remain to be answered. Most of Oklahoma's big, man-made lakes do not freeze shut in winter, and they are alive with fish. Many a Common Loon may winter on them, arriving with full-feathered wings and molting from January to March. Loons seen day after day in winter should be watched. When flightless birds "rouse" (i.e., stand in the water and flap their wings), the absence or shortness of wing-quills should be apparent.

Note that Virgil E. Dowell, on January 24, 1954, took from a net on Lake Texoma a winter-plumaged loon whose wing-quills were only partly grown. Note also that a stub-winged bird in gray feather caught on a bass plug in Grand Lake about June 1, 1950, was probably immature, for by June 1, adult Common Loons should be in breeding feather and on the breeding ground.

Cattle Egret

(Bubulcus ibis)

As a youngster I knew that the three really white kinds of herons that I might see were the Great Egret (*Casmerodius albus*), whose bill was yellow and whose legs and toes were black; the much smaller Snowy Egret (*Egretta thula*), with black legs and yellow toes; and the Little Blue Heron (*E. caerulea*), which was dark all over as an adult but white with pale gray wingtips and greenish gray legs and toes during its first year. If, in those early days, I had ever heard of a Cattle Egret, I suspected that it lived in some far away place, India perhaps, where cattle were said to be sacred.

Today, the Cattle Egret may well be the commonest heron of the southern Great Plains. I have no official counts to support this guess, but I know that since 1962 it has become common in many parts of Oklahoma; that its colonies are flourishing here; and that white herons seen away from water, whether among cattle or not, are likely to be Cattle Egrets. The species has a shape all its own. It does not often look long-necked. Its chin plumage extends forward under the basal half of the bill more than in other herons. When young it is white all over, when adult, white with a suffusion of orange-brown on crown, lower back, and chest. At the height of the breeding season the bill, legs, and feet of the adult are bright yellow.

Bubulcus ibis now inhabits all of the world's continents except Antarctica. Its spread has been outward in all directions from tropical Africa's wetlands—not, I hasten to say, from the rain forests there but from open country throughout which vast numbers of grazing mammals, water buffalo chiefly, live; successful reproduction has required trees, but not dense stands of timber, for the nests. Therefore,

7

breeding has started in the dry season, when grasshoppers provided sufficient food for both adults and small nestlings, and wound up in the wet season, when frogs, which breed then, are available for large nestlings about to fledge. The spread westward from Africa took the species to South America, where it was first noted between 1877 and 1882. From South America it has spread rapidly northward into North America.

Cattle Egrets of the southern Great Plains probably subsist chiefly on insects. In Oklahoma the species is migratory. It feeds largely in pastureland rather than along shores, thus filling an ecological niche that probably results in little competition with other herons. When nestlings become large and need more nourishment, heavier foods such as snakes, frogs, and small fish are available, but the parent birds continue to find food chiefly in open grassland where they are associated with cattle.

Watch the egrets as they feed. Keeping close to the heads and feet of the grazing animals, they snatch anything in the insect line that moves, chiefly grasshoppers and crickets. They sometimes alight on the cattle, a habit responsible for widespread belief that they prey on ticks and botfly larvae, thus repaying the cows for the help the big animals have given them in stirring up grasshoppers. Such a symbiotic relationship is probably more imagined than real, for I have never seen a Cattle Egret pecking at anything along the edges of a cow's ears or on the animal's back. The egrets like to hunt food in short grass. Insects that they find there may be destructive to what the cattle are eating, so to that limited extent the egrets help the cattle.

Somewhat amusing is the fact that adult Cattle Egrets, the very birds that slave away at keeping the nestlings properly fed, see to it that these young birds do not have the optimum position near a grazing cow. This best spot is the lowered head of the big mammal. Here the adult egrets watch for every insect that moves, and the young egrets are

8

Cattle Egret, *Bubulcus ibis*. Florida, 1980. Stephen H. Vaughan.

obliged to trail along—as best they may—as close as they can get to the cow's feet.

According to observations in Oklahoma dating back to 1962, it is the young Cattle Egrets, the pure white ones, that do most of the wandering away from the established colonies. The wandering probably takes place shortly after the young birds' major wing quills have reached full length and before the molt starts. How long a period this is has not yet been determined. When adult birds start to molt, flight-power may be reduced just enough to keep them from attempting protracted flight.

Mallard

Anas platyrhynchos

On June 13, 1980, at a large sewage pond near Boise City, at the west end of the Oklahoma Panhandle, John S. Shackford saw eight hen Mallards, each with a brood of small ducklings. He counted them all from one position. The broods ranged from one to eleven, a total of forty ducklings. Nowhere did he clearly see a drake Mallard in direct attendance to a hen with a brood. There is nothing scenic about those ponds. The whole countryside is flat and largely treeless. In the ponds are some cattails, and between the ponds are rank weeds. In the water there must be precisely the animal life that Mallard ducklings need.

A thoughtful person is not to be blamed for asking, "Where were the drakes, the handsome greenheads?" It is easy enough to say that among many duck species the drakes hang around during the egg-laying season and then depart, but that does not answer the question, nor does it put to rest curiosity about how many drakes might have been responsible for eight broods. The Mallard is believed to be monogamous. What a riot of color, splash, and sparkle that clutch of Boise City ponds must have been when all eight drakes were displaying before the hens!

Careful observers, hidden in blinds, can ascertain how many drakes consort with the hens at the Boise City sewage ponds, but finding out what the drakes do after egg-laying is over will require close attention. If they leave the area, when do they go, and what direction do they take? Do they establish bachelor quarters somewhere close by, or do they leave the area completely? There are not many marshes near Boise City and none of them appears to me to be better able than the ponds themselves to provide a

11

Mallard, *Anas platyrhynchos*. New Mexico, 1979. © Phillip Boyer/
National Audubon Society Collection, PR.

habitat for drake Mallards during that difficult late-summer
period when adult ducks lose all their wing feathers at
once, and the drakes molt into the somber, henlike, eclipse
plumage. Do the drakes stay at the ponds, but keep apart
from the hens and broods? The greenheads become brown-
heads somewhere, and I suspect that they are so secretive
while molting that they keep themselves out of sight. It
might take some real work to kick those dull-colored drakes
out of hiding among the weeds at the sewage ponds.

Another question might well be asked about Shackford's
sighting. Why the great difference in the size of the broods?
Hen Mallards lay large clutches—six to twelve eggs as a
rule. Then why a brood of only one duckling? Here the answer could be that some eggs never hatch, that some ducklings die at hatching, or that some are caught by predators.
The one-duckling broods are complete broods. The mother
duck does not return to the nest to hatch more eggs. Nor

will she consider the one-duckling brood a failure and abandon it or give it to another hen with a small brood and proceed with laying another clutch.

And how many of the forty ducklings will reach maturity? Here continuous watching might provide some kind of answer, for the broods will remain on the ponds with their mothers for about seven weeks while their wings develop enough for flight and while she herself goes through the flightless period of the late summer molt. All of them, mothers and broods alike, will gain their powers of flight at about the same time. If the sewage ponds are, in other words, adequate as a habitat for flightless adult hens and their broods, then why not also for adult drakes?

Sewage ponds like those at Boise City may be truly important as "production areas" for Mallards and other ducks, but at this moment no one knows how many ducklings hatched there reach maturity. Probably only a very few do. Predators include the snapping turtle, which may have established itself at the ponds and which approaches slowly from below, thrusts its head suddenly forward with jaws open, and clamps them shut on a duckling.

An important fact to bear in mind about the Mallard is that it is not far northern in distribution. It breeds widely, having an almost cosmopolitan breeding range in the North Temperate Zone, but there are large parts of the north country (e.g., the Labrador Peninsula) that have no Mallards in summer. At a big lake in Reykjavík, Iceland, there is a resident population of wild Mallards that everybody feeds. The drakes become flightless there while they wear the henlike eclipse plumage. Within most of the Mallard's range, the drakes probably move away from the breeding areas in what have been called "molt migrations." It is something of a mystery where the populations of molting drakes lose their handsome plumage, become henlike in color, and regain their flight powers.

13

Hooded Merganser

Lophodytes cucullatus

The hen Hooded Merganser and the drake in his seldom-seen dull eclipse plumage are surely among the least colorful of ducks; but the fully adult drake, in the high courtship dress that he wears all winter, is among the most truly ornamental of North American birds. The chief feature of that dress is the black-edged fan of pure white that he wears on his head.

The fan shuts down when he dives, so the white in it hardly shows, but when he comes up and shakes his head free of water, it suddenly flares; and we gasp as we look, partly at the sheer beauty of it all and partly because the fluffy dryness of the waterproof plumage is so unexpected. Not long ago, at one of central Oklahoma's big impoundments, I watched four drakes as they fed in water five or six feet deep not far offshore. They probably had flown to the spot in a flock, but while I watched they were so far apart and under water so much that it was hard to tell how many there were. One would pop to the surface, flare his crest, and float serenely. Another would pop up, several rods away, and I'd know there were two. Then a third would surface a split second after the first had gone under and I'd find myself wondering, sincerely wondering, how many there were. How fast could they swim under water? Not one of them brought a fish or frog up. What they caught must have been small and easy to swallow. All fish-eating ducks occasionally capture prey so large that they have trouble killing and swallowing it. Fish must, of course, be swallowed head first. The capturing is done under water, but killing and swallowing take time if the fish is large, so the killing and swallowing must be done on the surface, lest the captor drown.

I have never found a Hooded Merganser's nest, but my former student David F. Parmelee has found several. One that he found in Michigan's Upper Peninsula held a complete clutch of fourteen eggs. The nest was in a tree cavity well above ground. Getting to the eggs required cutting the tough wood away, for his arm was not long enough to reach them. The chopping took time. About half of the chips fell to the ground, the other half into the cavity. When, finally, he could reach the eggs, he felt first the chips that had accumulated, then, under them, the soft feathers of the hen merganser's back. Not once, during that long ordeal, had she attempted to leave those precious eggs.

The eggs were pure white, hard-shelled, and more nearly spherical than the eggs of most ducks. The clutch usually numbers eight to twelve eggs. Incubation is said to require thirty-one days.

In southeastern Michigan, on May 9, 1949, William A. Lunk and I watched a hen Hooded Merganser that we felt sure had a nest close by. She flew in wide circles through a wooded swamp in which there were many dead trees. As she passed overhead she repeated a rough guttural *caarr* every few seconds. She was obviously agitated. I waded out to certain trees in which there were cavities and did some climbing, but found nothing. We tried hiding, hoping that we would see her enter a cavity, but again no luck. Finally she headed for the heart of the swamp and we saw no more of her.

On two occasions in Oklahoma a hen Hooded Merganser has been seen with a brood of young—the first on May 8, 1977, on the Kerr Reservoir in far eastern Oklahoma, and the second on May 21, 1981, at the Salt Plains National Wildlife Refuge in north-central Oklahoma. At neither of these localities had anyone suspected that a Hooded Merganser might have a nest anywhere in the area. No one had seen a hen going to or leaving a cavity in a tree and, most important, no one had seen a displaying drake, or a drake and hen together, or a drake hanging around during the egg-laying period. We can but wonder whether insemination of the hen takes place long before

15

Hooded Merganser, *Lophodytes cucullatus*. Denver Zoo, Colorado, 1983. David A. Leatherman.

egg-laying begins, thus accounting for the absence of the drake while egg-laying is going on. We can but wonder, too, where the drake is during the month-long period in which the hen is on the eggs. He obviously has nothing to do with caring for the ducklings.

At neither of the two localities mentioned above have hen Hooded Mergansers with older ducklings in tow been observed by anyone. At neither of them have drakes in courtship display been observed. Indeed, *Lophodytes cucullatus* has not been recorded very often in spring (March 18 to May 30) anywhere in Oklahoma. Since the species breeds here, it should be seen until the young birds have reached the flying stage. But where are the adult drakes when they molt into eclipse plumage? Do they pass the flightless period of the molt in hidden-away places? Do they become highly inconspicuous during that difficult period through employing certain unreported tactics?

Turkey Vulture

Cathartes aura

While driving through the gentle hills of southwestern Pennsylvania on a summer day many years ago, I saw well ahead of me, and upslope, a Turkey Vulture flying so low that it roused my curiosity. All the vultures I had seen earlier that day had been flying high and soaring. This one was quartering, moving back and forth upwind, perhaps zeroing in on a carcass on or near the highway just ahead of me. Slowing down, I watched the bird as it suddenly held its wings high and alighted in the tall grass.

Parking the car off the highway, I did my best to see the vulture, but it was out of sight, hidden by the vegetation.

Turkey Vulture, *Cathartes aura*. Colorado, 1982.
David A. Leatherman.

17

Knowing about where it had alighted, I walked toward the spot. I was quite close to it when it flew up. There, sure enough, was a cottontail whose decomposed carcass the vulture had ripped open and started to eat. When I looked for the vulture, expecting to see it circling me, I could not see it anywhere. Going back to the car, I waited half an hour, but the vulture did not return to its meal.

I had been dead right, I told myself, in believing that vulture had found the dead rabbit through its ability to smell. But what did I know? What did I actually *know*? Had the bird, using its keen eyesight, seen brightly colored necrophagous beetles that were also zeroing in on the carcass? Had the swarm of blue bottle flies been big enough to be noticeable?

As I drove on, I reviewed as best I could the controversy that had been raging among ornithologists about the Turkey Vulture's olfactory powers. Some observers believed that the bird could not, despite its having large "perforate" nostrils, smell a thing. Others were sure that it could smell a little, but probably not much. I remembered so well the part of Frank Chapman's book *Life in an Air Castle* (1938) that dealt with experiments conducted by the author on noncaptive birds on Barro Colorado Island in Panama. Those experiments had been crude, but they had not inhibited the birds by forcing them to live "away from home" in strange places, and they had convinced Chapman that the vultures had a good sense of smell and that they used it daily in finding food. I remembered, too, the experiments conducted by Victor Coles at Cornell. Those experiments were all with captive birds and they had involved blindfolding, odd food containers, and such outrageous (though well thought-out) procedures that it was a wonder the birds survived. One experiment forced the birds to eat heavily salted food for forty-eight hours, to go without drinking water for the same period, and then to choose from two containers of "fresh" water, one of which had been treated with concentrated ammonia so powerful that, according to one of the students, it "made the poor birds shed tears," yet they drank readily from both containers. An unexpected finding was that the vultures preferred freshly killed chicks of barnyard fowl to decayed flesh. The experiments by the Coles were inconclusive. Coles came to believe through them that the vultures could smell, but that their olfactory powers were of less importance to them than their excellent vision.

In 1935, Kenneth E. Stager, Senior Curator of Ornithology of the Los Angeles County Museum, decided to do some zeroing-in of his own on the problem. His experiments started with placing a newspaper-wrapped badger carcass in the heart of a thick-foliaged creosote bush just after dawn and watching that bait throughout the day. In the afternoon of the second day, a lone turkey vulture was observed circling in the area. A gentle wind was blowing from the west, and the vulture sailed around the bait in decreasing circles until it landed about thirty feet up-wind from the bait-containing bush. The vulture walked back and forth in the up-wind area for several moments, then launched itself into the air and resumed its circling.

So what was I to believe from what I had just seen— that the vulture, just happening to be flying low, caught a whiff of the dead rabbit and followed through by quartering until it found the carcass? What if the vulture had not been flying low—would it have seen the carcass while soaring a thousand feet above it? The controversy continued to rage, as it were, within me.

Mississippi Kite

Ictinia mississippiensis

I spent several weeks in 1936 in west-central Oklahoma studying this handsome raptor, so I know a good deal about its habits and behavior. Though it dived at me fiercely, squealing its shrill *phee-phew* whenever I climbed to its nests, I came to think of it as a gentle bird, a consummate master of flight, a lover of summer, whatever that season might have to offer. How often have I seen a pair, newly arrived from their far-removed wintering ground to the south, perched peacefully in the thin shade of a locust tree, simply idling. Last year's flimsy nest might be quite usable again, what with the addition of a few twigs; in-

Mississippi Kite, *Ictinia mississippiensis*. Kansas, 1970.
James W. Parker.

20

sects galore are to be captured without much effort; the world of shelter-belts, scrubby "shinnery" oak, and stream-side cottonwoods is theirs to enjoy.

It is, in other words, something of a surprise when I learn, through officers of an Oklahoma City country club, that the kites have been attacking people so savagely that the Oklahoma Department of Wildlife Conservation has been asked to "do something about it," and when, in a letter from southwestern Oklahoma, I am told of a kite that struck a woman's head, snatching off her hair-net. The slightly dazed woman had wondered, quite understandably, what her attacker was carrying off in its talons.

Day after day, during that memorable season with the kites, I climbed to their nests, most of which were less than thirty feet from the ground, recording data having to do with the incubation period, food brought to very young chicks, and the behavior of young birds while fledging. One nest, at the edge of a clump of "shinnery" (a cowboy's word for chênier, the French word for oak), was so low that on horseback I could approach almost to within touching distance of the brooding bird without frightening it off. How piercingly bright were those red eyes that seemed to be expressing the bird's wonder as to why this particular horse should be different from other horses.

The kite's feet are small, its legs short. It does not look for prey from a perch, but rather while flying. I have never seen a kite on the ground or, for that matter, on a low rock, bush, or fencepost. If the nest is only eight to ten feet up, the birds alight there, of course, but they shun perches lower than that. They snatch prey from the ground—lizards, small mammals, small snakes, mole crickets, tarantulas, lubber grasshoppers—killing and perhaps eating it while flying. I have never seen a kite carrying really heavy prey, such as a full-grown cotton rat.

Most nests that I visited in 1936 held two eggs. These were laid about forty-eight hours apart and were incubated (by both sexes) for a little over a month. The skin of the ventral apterium was more highly vascularized in females than in males, so I decided that the females did most

21

of the incubating. I did not learn which sex spent the night on the nest. Newly hatched chicks were fed soft parts of insects, chiefly grasshoppers. Fledging took a little over a month. I found little evidence that the birds preyed on birds, mammals, or reptiles; but in other parts of Oklahoma many small rodents, small lizards, and such birds as Chimney Swifts are captured. Remains found under a nest-tree in the Tulsa area, where the kite is not common, included feathers of recently fledged Purple Martins.

At certain bat caves near Reed, southwestern Oklahoma, and at Vickery's Cave in Major County, northwestern Oklahoma, the kites prey regularly on free-tailed bats, visiting the cave entrances in the gloaming and catching bats as the hordes pour out.

The Mississippi Kite has extended its breeding range westward almost to the New Mexico state line within the past half-century. Throughout the Panhandle it lives in woods along the larger streams. Where one pair nests there are likely to be other pairs close by. A few pairs now nest regularly along the Cimarron near the Black Mesa.

One fact about this strongly migratory bird interests me greatly: it manages to avoid cold weather. It arrives, often in flocks, in late spring and departs for its winter home while the weather still is warm-to-hot. According to my summary of records, most Mississippi Kites have left Oklahoma by the end of September, a few are still present in the first week of October, and sightings during the rest of October are exceptional. One wonders whether a sudden drop in air temperature would actually kill the birds. Drastic weather changes are part of life in the southern Great Plains.

The kites that nest on well-manicured country club grounds are of special interest to me. Many insects that the kites prey on cannot be numerous where the grass is mowed regularly. Cicadas are available in season, of course, and big dragonflies may be commoner than we realize. Do the kites prey heavily on small birds in such areas? A careful study of an urbanized population might bring to light some highly significant facts.

22

Bald Eagle

Haliaeetus leucocephalus

There is something funny—as well as heartwarming—about beholding the majestic obliged to deal with the unmajestic. A world-famous contralto, whose trailing dress catches on a splinter as she approaches center stage, has to pull that dress free without creating a scene. A great nation's president, who stumbles as he descends from an aircraft, has to proceed as if nothing untoward has happened. Seeing fellow human beings cope with such problems is, I say, heartwarming.

Early one spring morning in Columbus, Ohio, Ed Thomas took me to a birding spot of which he was fond. We had—as I remember it all—been listening to the song of a Lincoln's Sparrow (*Melospiza lincolnii*). Suddenly, out of the blue, came an adult Bald Eagle that seemed twice its natural size because it was so close. It alighted near the end of the longest branch in a dead tree, looked us over, and started to preen its plumage. Again suddenly, and this time very suddenly indeed, a small black bird, probably a grackle, descended, struck the eagle hard on the head, and darted off. The eagle, trying to avoid the blow, dodged with its whole massive body; we heard a sound of cracking, and down went half of the dead tree, eagle and all. The eagle, with legs stuck out, claws open, and wings flapping awkwardly, decided not to trust what was left of the tree and flew off. But it did so majestically.

Never have I been closer than I was that day to a wild, free-flying Bald Eagle, nor closer to a Bald Eagle's nest than the foot of a nest-tree. I have, however, seen a good deal of the species in Florida, on Vancouver Island in Alaska, and, surprisingly enough, in Oklahoma. The big man-made lakes in Oklahoma are teeming with fish, and truly sizable

Bald Eagle, *Haliaeetus leucocephalus*, subadult. Oklahoma, 1974.
John S. Shackford.

winter populations of Bald Eagles have built up here during the last forty or fifty years. James W. Lish, who has focused his attention upon the eagles during the past decade, estimates that six hundred Bald Eagles winter regularly in Oklahoma.

Most of these wintering eagles spend their time along the shores of the big impoundments. They feed on fish primarily, but catch some waterfowl. James L. Norman has observed them catching fish that have made their way up the Neosho River below the Fort Gibson Reservoir dam when the water was high and were trapped in shallow pools when the water subsided. Lish found that in the tallgrass prairie of Osage County, Oklahoma, the eagles fed largely on the carcasses of cattle that died during bad weather.

The Bald Eagle may have nested along the Cimarron in far western Oklahoma and along the Arkansas in northeastern Oklahoma about the turn of the century, but the nestings were not documented. In 1950 a pair summered in northeastern Oklahoma, but did not nest. About that same time a pair built a nest in a huge sycamore along the west side of Fort Gibson Reservoir, but they reared no young. A communal roost that existed from December to early March built up at Grand Lake in the state's northeasternmost corner between 1945 and 1960. Most of the birds at that roost were immature.

At the Robert S. Kerr Reservoir in far eastern Oklahoma one pair of eagles did not leave the area with the rest of the wintering population in the early spring of 1977, but remained to nest. Just when the nest was built no one knows. It might have been built and used in 1976 or 1975, though no one reported finding it during those years. Once the U.S. Army Corps of Engineers learned that eagles were using it, they guarded it zealously, keeping boats away, urging motorists on the highway to keep moving, and finally, on July 2, having the satisfaction of seeing one young eagle safely out of the nest. Whether the eaglet could fly on that date is questionable. Not until July 9 did they see it well away from the nest-tree (L.D. Isley, 1979, *Bull. Oklahoma Ornithol. Soc.,* 12: 1–4). At that same nest, eagles reared another young one in 1981. How many eggs were laid in 1977 and 1981 no one knows, for orders against climbing to the nest or bothering the birds in any other way were strict.

No one knows whether the very same two eagles raised the young bird in 1977 and 1981. It is known, however, that eagles become attached to a spot at which they have bred successfully. Shortly after the young bird fledged in 1981, a strong wind blew nest and nest-tree down. The Corps of Engineers promptly erected a platform of the same height as the nest-tree and all hands are watching it with great interest.

To be borne in mind is the probability that the eagles will not always raise young there every year. No one should be discouraged if they do not build the nest on the plat-form every year. But how very gratifying if this, our national bird, can be induced to breed regularly in Oklahoma![1]

[1] *Editorial note:* In 1982, fifty miles southwest of Kerr Reservoir, a single pair of Bald Eagles successfully raised two young; no other successful nestings are known in Oklahoma for the period 1982–85.

Northern Harrier

Circus cyaneus

Whatever the time of year, this lanky, slender-bodied raptor—which is known in England as the Hen Harrier and which has for centuries been called the Marsh Hawk in the United States—is easy to identify from its characteristic habit of looking for prey while quartering back and forth a few feet above the ground in open country. Almost never does it fly into or through the woods. Almost never does it perch on a telephone pole or high branch. Having captured prey, it may alight on a fencepost long enough to tear apart and consume the mouse or frog, but never does it stay there for a rest after eating. In this refusal to idle awhile, with tail down and plumage fluffed out, it differs radically from most hawks. Its rump is white—noticeably so. Adult males are gray, adult females brown, young birds in first winter feather even browner.

In early spring on its nesting ground the harrier's flight can be downright spectacular. Now, as if suddenly possessed, the male hurls himself into a wild flurry of loop-the-loops, cackling loudly while he performs, obviously eager to impress his mate. Female birds are said to loop-the-loop too, but I have never seen one doing it. As for the species' custom of circling high in the air—behavior I have witnessed from time to time—I have no explanation.

The Northern Harrier nests widely in North America, from the south edge of the tundra in Alaska and Canada southward throughout most of the United States. I was surprised to find it common in fall at the Partridge Creeks, along the shore of James Bay, in 1923 and 1926. Most birds that I saw there day after day were brown young-of-the-year. They did most of their hunting not on the vast mud-

27

Northern Harrier, *Circus cyaneus*. California, 1965.
Velma Harris, F.P.S.A.

flats, which were teeming with shorebirds, but in the
bulrushes-and-sedge area that lay between willows and
flats. What they were capturing I did not ascertain. One
that I flushed had been eating a full-grown American Black
Duck (*Anas rubripes*), but I had no proof that the hawk had
killed such large prey.

Nests are on the ground, usually in areas not often visited by human beings. In Oklahoma, nests have been
found in a wide variety of places. Two that Karl W. Haller
and I found in 1937 at the east end of the Panhandle were
among cattails in a marshy strip paralleling the Cimarron
River. Four found in 1956 by Vaud A. Travis, Jr., in the Jackson Bay area just west of Fort Gibson Reservoir, were in
dry prairie. One found in 1940 by Paul F. Nighswonger
near Alva was in a wild plum thicket well away from water.
It held three eggs on June 2, five eggs on June 9, and four
chicks (which he banded) on July 21. He discovered that
nest by seeing the female bird fly up from it to receive,
midair, prey brought by the male. A nest that Lawrence E.
Dunn showed me on June 30, 1961, was in a wheatfield in

Harper County. A small pond nearby doubtless furnished the family (three large young) with frogs and snakes. Nests found recently in Cimarron County by William G. Voelker were in dry prairie not far from a large, shallow, alkaline pond.

During the early part of the month-long fledging period the male captures most of the prey for the brood. But as the chicks become larger the mother bird has to provide some of the food, so during that part of the summer both parents range widely in their hunting and often bring to the nest sizable prey such as large snakes, rabbits, and good-sized birds. Harriers do not, according to my observations, eat many insects.

A prey item that has puzzled me is worth discussing. At Pymatuning Swamp, in northwestern Pennsylvania, where several pairs of the hawks nested in 1922, I observed a male bird carrying a small mammal to a fallen dead tree. Using the binocular, I watched the hawk nibble at what it held in its foot, then fly off, carrying nothing. Curious, I waded out to the dead tree and found lying there, just as the hawk had left it, a star-nosed mole (*Condylura cristata*), the first I had ever seen in the flesh. Was the hawk merely surfeited with food, or was the mole distasteful?

Another question: Why, during my past thirty years in Oklahoma have I never seen a Northern Harrier looping-the-loop? I have been afield a great deal, and all over the state at all seasons. Do the birds loop-the-loop only in the northern part of their range? Do they not loop-the-loop unless several pairs are nesting close together? Environmentalists may argue that I have never seen looping-the-loop here because marshes have been destroyed right and left as rivers have been impounded and big lakes formed. The face of the countryside has indeed been changing, what with the construction of highways, and the raising of crops, but to be remembered is the fact that most harriers that nest in Oklahoma nest in prairie-land, not in marshes.

Broad-winged Hawk

Buteo platypterus

The broadwing is such a mild-mannered, undemonstrative hawk that a pair may occupy a shady corner of the woods all summer without anyone knowing they are there. The species ranges widely in continental North America and the West Indies, breeding northward to Alberta, Saskatchewan, Manitoba, Ontario, Quebec, Nova Scotia, and New Brunswick and southward to Texas, the Gulf coast, and Florida. In Oklahoma it breeds chiefly in eastern and central counties, though it has several times been seen as far west as the New Mexico state line. It gathers in flocks as it moves southward in fall, and winters in Central America and northern South America. December records for the southern Great Plains are questionable, though some broadwings do winter regularly in Florida.

The species returns in spring without fanfare, builds its inconspicuous nest, and proceeds to raise two or three young. I suspect that many pairs form in winter or during northward migration, for I have seen very little circling high in the sky or showing-off among recently arrived birds. The broadwing's loudest cries are curiously thin, high, and feeble, often sounding not at all like those of a bird of prey. A cry that I heard over and over in West Virginia one spring was so much like that of a wood-pewee that I actually misidentified the hawk until—wholly by accident—I found its nest.

Nesting in Oklahoma usually begins in April. A nest found by William A. Carter in the southeastern corner of the state on March 27, 1964, might well have been built and used the year before. An adult broadwing was standing on it. An empty nest found April 18, 1954, in central Okla-

30

homa was still empty on April 25, though on both dates the old birds were close by. A nest found April 26, 1936, in northeastern Oklahoma held three eggs, a full clutch. One found in south-central Oklahoma by W. Michael Brewer on May 20, 1967, held three small chicks on May 28. It was in a blackjack oak only fifteen feet from the ground and was lined with leaves. One found in southeastern Oklahoma by William A. Carter on June 19, 1961, in a shortleaf pine forty feet up, held two downy chicks. A young bird barely able to fly was cornered and photographed in northeastern Oklahoma by Sophia C. Mery on July 5, 1966. Three young birds, barely able to fly and still being fed by their parents, were seen by William Talbert in southwestern Oklahoma on July 5, 1974.

In south-central Oklahoma, where I taught a course in bird study during several summers, my students and I knew that widely scattered pairs of broadwings were nesting in mature woodlands just north of Lake Texoma, yet we found no nests. The best looks we had at adult birds were along roads where the hawks watched for prey as it moved into the open. We had a wonderful look from our cars at one bird that tried to catch a snake at the edge of the highway. It was only thirty feet or so from us, flopping around in the weeds trying to get a firm grip. At first we thought it was crippled. Then we saw the three-foot writhing reptile held by the powerful talons. The snake may have been too big for the hawk, or perhaps our stopping to watch frightened the hawk. At any rate, it dropped the snake and flew off.

The broadwing is not a rapid flyer. It rarely, if ever, preys on birds. It is a confirmed eater of insects, having a special fondness for the larvae of certain large moths. The stomach contents of two young birds collected on August 20, 1959, and September 12, 1964, were, respectively, a mass of grasshopper and cicada remains, and eight large grasshoppers that had been swallowed whole.

In a park-like area just east of the university campus in Norman, I observed an adult broadwing repeatedly between August 29 and September 2, 1954. Obviously, it was

Broad-winged Hawk, *Buteo platypterus*. Ontario, Canada, 1981.
James M. Richards.

finding food along a small stream there. On September 2 it
was perched well up in a willow close to a low bridge that
crossed the stream. It was looking intently not at me but at
the ground under it. Suddenly, quite heedless of my presence, it flew down to a leafy branch that the wind had recently wrenched from the willow, grasped the butt end,
and flew up carrying the unwieldy burden to a higher
perch. Then, refusing to drop what it carried, it flew across
the stream to a sycamore. I expected to see it picking cater-
pillars from the branch, but it did no such thing. Again it
flew, this time across the street to a big elm. Finally, still
carrying that willow branch, it flew off through the trees
and out of sight. What it could have wanted with the
branch was quite beyond me. Was it testing the strength of
its talons? Was it merely playing?

Red-tailed Hawk

Buteo jamaicensis

The Red-tailed Hawk breeds widely in Oklahoma and is fairly common in summer. Its ecology at that season is interesting. In some low-lying woodlands of eastern and central Oklahoma, areas that are subject to flooding, it is less common than the Red-shouldered Hawk (*B. lineatus*), a species that feeds heavily on semi-aquatic prey. In the Panhandle, especially in Texas County and the eastern three-fourths of Cimarron County, it is less common than the Ferruginous Hawk (*B. regalis*), which nests in trees in that area. In the Black Mesa country it is hardly even a woodland bird: every redtail nest that I have seen there has been on a cliff.

The geographical race of the redtail that breeds in Oklahoma is *Buteo jamaicensis fuertesi*, a form characterized by the comparatively unmarked underparts of the adult. Like the so-called eastern redtail (*B. jamaicensis borealis*), *fuertesi*

Red-tailed Hawk, Harlan's race, *Buteo jamaicensis harlani*. Oklahoma, 1984. John S. Shackford.

33

has no dark (melanistic) phase. Among the many pairs of breeding redtails that I have observed in Oklahoma during the past fifty years, not a single bird has been melanistic. To my surprise, however, I have found that young birds raised here often are quite heavily marked with brownish black on the belly in their first winter plumage.

Nests of redtails in Oklahoma are usually well up in large trees, and nest-trees are sometimes close to mankind's roads and buildings. At Doby Springs in Harper County, just east of the Panhandle, a nest that has been used for years is sixty feet up in a large tree only a stone's throw from the front porch of a farmhouse. The farmer raises chickens. "Do the hawks bother the chickens?" I ask. "No," comes the reply, "I guess the hawks find all the rabbits and rats they need out a ways from the house. They leave the chickens be, even the little ones."

The redtail is much commoner in winter than in summer in Oklahoma, for during the colder months several geographical races move in from more northern parts of the continent. The advent of these outsiders does not oblige the breeding population to leave, so adult and young redtails that vary greatly in appearance are to be seen along all highways in winter. One reason the hawks are so much in evidence is that where the traffic moves swiftly much animal life is killed, and the hawks, opportunists all, let the traffic do their killing for them. Any motorist out early in the morning sees hawks on or near the roads—especially the paved ones—eating what has been struck by cars the night before.

Darkest of the redtail's several subspecies is *B. jamaicensis harlani*, a northwestern form long thought to be a full species and known as Harlan's Hawk. Adult and immature male and female *harlani* are dark, even black-looking at a distance, except when, taking flight, they show the partly gray tail. The tail feathers of *harlani* are highly variable, some being barred with black, herring-bone style, some having odd and beautiful longitudinal markings, some being tinged with red. One *harlani* that I watched all winter near Norman had several almost white feathers in its gray tail, a pattern that made the bird instantly recognizable as an individual. Another feature of *harlani* is the largely concealed white plumage of the throat and chest, a whiteness that does not show at all clearly in the field as a rule.

The late Craig M. Lowe, a young man who loved the birds of prey, made a careful study of the breeding redtails of central Alaska during the last few years of his life. He was puzzled by mixed pairs that he found, one of which consisted of an average all-dark *harlani* and a richly colored bird that he felt represented one of the more southward ranging races. This richly colored individual had an all-red tail. When Craig told me of the mixed pair, I could not help thinking of the many Harlan's redtails that I had seen in central and eastern Oklahoma. While driving eastward from Norman, I had been impressed winter after winter with the numbers of all-black birds that were perched on poles along the highways. With them were, of course, occasional richly-colored birds and birds with unmarked underparts, but the all-blacks seemed to be the commonest.

What did I *know* about the forces that would send the all-black birds back to their breeding grounds in British Columbia and Alaska at winter's end? Was mere lengthening of days the most important of them? Might hostility of light-colored redtails about to breed in Oklahoma be one? To what extent had the urge to reproduce been a force? Had courtship been going on among the wintering birds, behavior that no one had noticed? Had pairs actually formed in Oklahoma?

Suddenly I found myself thinking that pairing might well take place among wintering populations of redtails, pairing that would be consummated not here in Oklahoma but en route to, and on, the northern nesting grounds. I decided that wintering redtails should be watched with this thought in mind. If pairing goes on among wintering populations, no wonder some of the redtail's several races are endlessly variable.

35

Ferruginous Hawk

Buteo regalis

So named from the rusty tone of dark parts of its plumage, this is North America's largest, most eagle-like buteo. It inhabits wide open, wind-swept country along the western edge of the Great Plains, in some areas nesting exclusively in places difficult to climb to on cliffs, buttresses, and rocky pinnacles, in other areas principally in trees but sometimes on the ground. It preys on ground squirrels, pocket gophers, and prairie dogs chiefly, but also on cottontails and jack rabbits, bullsnakes, and an occasional bird. Its long, powerful legs are feathered down to the toes. Females, which are larger than males, have a wingspread of four and a half feet.

The species comes in three color phases—a light, a dark reddish brown, and a black. Adult light-phased birds are brown on the upperparts except for the tail, which is white, and white below except for the rust-colored legs. Some, perhaps all, young light-phased birds are white rather than rusty on the legs. Dark birds are, generally speaking, brown all over, the red-phased (erythristic) ones having a rufous tone, the very dark (melanistic) ones a blackish tone. Whatever the individual's color-phase, its underwings are pale and its tail unbarred. Too, there is an area at the base of the primaries through which sunlight passes, creating a fairly dependable fieldmark if the bird is flying. Tail color in dark birds varies greatly, in some individuals being almost white, in others gray.

The big hawk watches for prey less often from a treetop, pole, or the sky than from the ground. Often it hunts in pairs. Perched on old mounds along the edge of a prairie dog town, the two birds wait until one of the dogs wan-

36

ders a long way from its burrow, then, flying in swiftly, they intercept its return to the burrow, force it to run this way and that in its confusion, and pin it down.

At mounds of fresh earth brought to the surface by a pocket gopher, one of the hawks waits patiently until movement of the earth tells it that the gopher is returning, whereupon, plunging its foot deep into the loose earth, it grabs its prey.

Oklahoma birds seen by me in summer between 1936 and 1978 were, without exception, of the light phase. Dark birds apparently are common along the north edge of the range, and these show up in great numbers in western Oklahoma in winter. I recall driving from Boise City in Cimarron County to the Texas state line on February 9, 1955, and seeing—on poles close to the highway—literally scores of Ferruginous Hawks, most of them of a dark color phase.

Ferruginous Hawk, *Buteo regalis*, light and dark color phases. Oklahoma, 1982. John S. Shackford.

My first Oklahoma nest of the Ferruginous Hawk I found on March 29, 1959, near Guymon, in the Panhandle. It was in the one tree, a small, bushy one, that stood in the middle of a vast field a hundred yards from a much-used highway. About half finished, it was only twelve feet from the ground and so was easy to reach. Among the stuff that the birds had used in building the four-foot wide structure were old rags, paper napkins, and trampled stalks of tumbleweed. Both birds screamed *kee-ah* loudly while I was at the nest, but neither attacked me. While I was watching from my car, one of them brought in the sleeve of a brightly colored shirt. On April 2, when I visited the nest again, it appeared to be finished, but neither bird was in sight anywhere. Egg-laying apparently had not yet started.

William G. Voelker, who has focused his attention on the Ferruginous Hawks of Oklahoma, has found many nests, all of them in trees. Year after year he has observed pairs in which both birds were light-phased, and he has banded many young, all of them light-phased. But in 1981, just south of Felt, a town near the Texas state line in Cimarron County, he found a mixed pair, the big female melanistic, the male light-phased. At that pair's nest (in a living hackberry, fourteen feet from the ground) five young were reared, each melanistic like the mother. In 1982 the pair at that nest again was mixed, the female being melanistic, and the three young reared again were black like the mother.

I'd have predicted that each of those broods would be mixed, but no: the genes of the dark female prevailed during *both* nestings! May we now expect mixed pairs all over that part of the state? When watching the handsome birds, we cannot help thinking: assuming the "survival of the fittest" is indeed a valid concept, why should light, red, and black birds go on producing light, red, and black young? Is each phase *equally* able to survive? Or does the continuing existence of the species actually depend on the continuing existence of the three phases? More must be learned about melanistic birds.

American Kestrel

Falco sparverius

One day in late spring the campus tree surgeons brought to my third-floor office at Cornell University four baby American Kestrels. They were in a gunny sack, one dead, the others on their backs with talons and beaks ready for attack. The nest-cavity in which they had hatched was in a dead tree that had just been felled. They were frightened and defiant, but a little petting and talking-to calmed them down.

They're hungry, I thought, as I removed the dead one. Having at hand a small bird whose skin had recently been prepared for my research collection, I cut strips of meat, dangled these above the three hooked beaks and six black eyes, and was not greatly surprised when all three babies opened their mouths wide and squealed *killee, killee, killee* in a chorus so loud that everyone in the building heard it. They had called without getting to their feet. Indeed, as they lay there, looking as if done-for, I wondered if their backs had been broken. Then one of them nibbled at the meat, seized it, wolfed it down and suddenly all three were sitting on their heels, looking fierce, gulping eagerly, and looking for more.

The handsome little falcons fared well. No one tried to tame or train them. The tufts of white down that clung to their head plumage soon disappeared. In a few weeks, when able to fly well, all were taken to open country that was alive with grasshoppers and liberated.

Once known as the American Sparrow Hawk—an unsuitable name, since a rounded-winged, middle-sized bird-catching hawk of the Old World has for centuries been called the Sparrow Hawk in England—*Falco sparverius* is a

39

New World species that ranges northward almost to tree-limit and southward to Tierra del Fuego. It breeds widely in the southern Great Plains, being found in summer not only in rural areas but in towns and cities. It nests in cavities in trees, in holes in cliffs, about the iron-work of bridges, and in crevices about buildings. In Oklahoma and Texas it is much more noticeable in winter than in summer, an abundance that may be explained partly by the influx of birds from the north but chiefly by the fact that breeding pairs are so secretive while rearing their young.

Nesting in towns proceeds so quietly that no one knows the birds are coming and going. A pair that bred in Norman, Oklahoma, in 1980 had their eyrie in the attic of a three-story building close to the university campus. Jack D. Tyler and I spent hours observing the old birds and their young. Not once were we attacked. Not once did we hear either old bird call. They came and went so unobtrusively that not a soul stopped to watch them.

What the old birds brought in as food was of real interest, for most of it was House Sparrows (*Passer domesticus*). We had fully expected it to be grasshoppers and mice chiefly, for that was what the books all said kestrels lived on. The old birds brought in sparrow after sparrow. The male seemed to do most of the hunting and all of his trips for prey seemed to take him southwestward from the nest. How far he went we did not ascertain. His mate spent much of her time at one corner of the flat roof of an eleven-floor building just across the street. Here she waited for the male, took prey from him, and plucked it. We could see the feathers scattering in the wind. The male did no plucking while we were watching him, but he did, on one occasion, take a featherless bird of sparrow-size to the nest, and this he may have plucked himself.

When the two eyases showed signs of eagerness to fledge, there was no fanfare. One hot day we saw them at the hole through which their parents had carried food. They were panting. We knew they would soon be flying. Within a day or so they were out, perched side by side atop a building across the street.

40

American Kestrel, *Falco sparverius*. California, 1960.
Velma Harris, F.P.S.A.

Jack and I became convinced that the kestrels were depending on the one prey species that was properly nourishing, easy to see and hear, and readily obtainable. Sparrows were almost ubiquitous in town. One prey item that the male brought in and that the female plucked, might have been a young Northern Mockingbird (*Mimus polyglottos*), for that day we saw an adult mocker diving at the kestrels while they were together on the high building's roof. We saw one kestrel catch something in midair—perhaps a dragonfly. One item that was brought in was very long and slender—perhaps a lizard or small snake.

While I was watching the male, he suddenly dropped from the high building and caught a sparrow right in front of me—one of a flock that was flying not far above the street on its way to a parking area in which bits of "fast food" might have been tossed from cars. Flying at its swiftest, that sparrow could not have matched the speed of the little falcon's stoop.

Snowy Plover

Charadrius alexandrinus

On a map, the blank space west of the main reservoir on the Great Salt Plains National Wildlife Refuge in north-central Oklahoma looks unexceptional enough. But walk eastward across the salt-encrusted flat there on a hot summer day, and your feelings become a mixture of wonder, disbelief, and apprehension. Never have you been in a place like this. When you are halfway to the edge of the big reservoir, the prairie is a long way behind you. That which sparkles just ahead is mirage, not water, for heat waves keep the reservoir out of sight until you are almost wading in it. In every direction the horizon has receded, now being pale, purplish, and barely visible. The thin layer of salt reminds you of an early snowfall, but the heat tells you clearly enough that nothing white hereabouts can be snow. You have been following a shallow stream called Clay Creek. To your surprise, there has been no quicksand.

In this harsh environment the Snowy Plover spends the summer and breeds successfully. It is a quiet, inconspicuous species at all seasons, but especially so on its nesting ground. So pale is the gray of its upperparts that unless it moves it is almost invisible. When it does move, it runs swiftly for several yards, stops abruptly, and snatches up a shore-fly (*Ephydra* sp.) or burrowing beetle (*Bledius* sp.), both of which are abundant. Its strides while running may measure up to six inches each. When flying, it does not spread its wings very wide. It is most noticeable when, flushed from a nest, it creeps along with wings fluttering or falls on its side with tail spread wide and one wing waving. It is an expert at feigning injury.

Obviously, the species finds plenty to eat on the salt

43

flats. Its system may not need strictly fresh water. Its nests are not hidden by vegetation, for there is no vegetation, but often they are near a rock, a bit of driftwood, or other debris. While objects of this sort provide some shelter from the wind, which can be fierce enough to blow eggs out of nests, they also attract wandering coyotes (*Canis latrans*). Some protection is afforded the plovers by two other birds that share the flats with them, the American Avocet (*Recurvirostra americana*) and the Least Tern (*Sterna antillarum*), both of which are noisy and aggressive in defending their own nests and young. Shade for the plover eggs is provided by the parent birds. Both sexes incubate the eggs and brood the chicks. Why only three eggs? The question is not pointless, for many species of the plover family lay four eggs. Has keeping four eggs at the proper temperature during the twenty-some day incubation period not worked out—as it obviously has for the Killdeer (*Charadrius vociferus*)? Thought-provoking is the fact that the three water-loving birds that nest together on the flats differ in clutch-size, the avocet laying four eggs, the Snowy Plover three (sometimes only two), the Least Tern two. The reason for this is not obvious.

A further comparative study of the three species is in order. To be borne in mind is the fact that the habits of the three differ markedly. Adult avocets feed largely while wading, sweeping their bills from side to side through the mud. The plovers find food at the water's edge and also at considerable distances away from it. The terns dive for their food, small fish. Young avocets may, for all I know, feed on flies and beetles before their bills start to recurve; if they do, they compete with the plovers, but not with the terns.

Scattered pairs of Snowy Plovers nest elsewhere in Oklahoma, chiefly on low-lying banks of rivers and impoundments, but I hazard the guess that more pairs nest in the "harsh" area discussed above than in all other parts of the state combined. Two recent observers, Paul B. Grover and his wife Mida, estimate that 325 pairs nested on the

Snowy Plover, *Charadrius alexandrinus*. Oklahoma, 1977.
Wesley S. Isaacs.

flats in 1977. That year forty-six pairs of avocets and thirty
pairs of Least Terns also nested there, all three species
tending to nest near water.

The Grovers believed that only 260 pairs of plovers
nested on the flats in 1978. That summer, on May 31, the
area was devastated by a severe rain-and-hail storm that
destroyed scores of nests of all three species. On the morning of June 1, eighteen adult plovers were found dead near
nests.

The Snowy Plover is currently believed to be a pale geographical race of the wide-ranging species that is represented in much of Europe by the bird known in England as
the Kentish Plover. This Kentish Plover so often tramples
the wet sand with its feet, thus bringing food to the surface, that several writers have discussed the habit in detail.
No one has reported observing the Snowy Plover obtaining food in this way. I must confess that I have not spent
much time watching the snowies feeding. I've spent a lot
of time looking for their nests, some of which were a long
way from the water's edge.

Killdeer

Charadrius vociferus

This member of the plover family is among the best known of American birds. Every farmer has been amused by its broken-wing tactics as it does its best to draw attention away from its eggs. Golfers have noticed that a bird with two black bars across its white breast frequents the fairways and greens. "Pretty bird, that," they say, familiar with it but not knowing its name.

Although classified as a shorebird, the Killdeer spends much of its life away from water. It feeds with sandpipers and plovers of other species on the mudflats, to be sure; but it usually nests well away from lakes and ponds, almost as if experience has taught it that high, well-drained places are safer than those close to water. I have seen many Killdeer nests in various parts of North America, and most of them have been in high dry areas that are receiving mankind's attentions in one way or another. One nest that I visited daily in central Oklahoma was at the edge of a gravel road about five feet from the shallow rut made by passing wheels. Another Oklahoma nest was in the middle of a dirt road used by cars rather than horse-drawn vehicles, another only a pebble's toss from second base of a baseball diamond, another in the very middle of a prairie dog town a long way from the closest farm pond.

Nests are described as "mere depressions in the ground," but I know that many of them are carefully lined with bits of gravel and small pebbles and I suspect that every nest represents a ritualistic making of two or three "scrapes," and a selecting of one for the eggs. A nest that I found in northwestern Pennsylvania in the spring of 1922 was in a flat area that had been burned-over. The "scrape" that the birds finally selected was so neatly lined with

46

pebbles and little chunks of charcoal that I knew the birds had worked hard over it. The smallest pebbles were in the very bottom of the shallow cup, the largest on the rim, and the nest was surrounded by pavement made largely of pieces of charcoal of so much the same size that they must have been selected with care.

I have yet to see a Killdeer's nest on a graveled roof, but I know that many a Killdeer chick has been hatched there and I wonder how the little thing gets to the ground. I suspect that it makes its way to the edge and falls off. But what if the roof has a retaining wall? Does the parent bird seize the chick and fly with it over the obstruction, then drop or carry it to the ground? And what about the important interim between hatching and departure from the nest? Do the parent birds bring water to the chicks? So far as I know, no one has ever witnessed hatching at a rooftop nest or descent to the ground of a rooftop chick.

The chicks are wonderfully tough in some ways, but fragile in others. They probably fall from the roof and hit the ground without hurting themselves in the least. But they cannot stand too much hot sun. Shading them while they are very young may, for all I know, be more important to their well-being than providing them with water.

How beautiful that chick is! It has two features worth discussing. Instead of two dark rings (and one white) around its neck it has a single dark one, and it has a tail of down that is remarkably long. When the molt into first winter plumage takes place, the one dark ring of barbless down-feathers (neossoptiles) is replaced by two dark rings of well-formed, barbed feathers (teleoptiles). But which dark ring of that first winter plumage—the upper or the lower—replaces the dark ring of the chick, or do *white* feathers replace it? Bird student though I am, and have been for a long time, I cannot answer this question. Stranger things happen every day in the bird world than the replacement of dark feathers with white ones during molt.

As for the long tail of the chick, these down feathers are pushed out by the incoming rectrices of the first winter plumage. The longest of the down feathers sometimes

Killdeer, *Charadrius vociferus*, feigning injury. Ontario, Canada, 1982. James M. Richards.

cling to the tips of the middle pair of first-winter rectrices until the remains of them wear away. In a specimen collected on July 28, 1951, along the shore of Lake Texoma in south-central Oklahoma, barbless down-feather remains that were almost an inch long clung to one middle rectrix. Small though such a feature is, it should be quite perceptible through a good binocular, and it instantly identifies its wearer as a bird under a year old.

The word Killdeer is obviously onomatopoeic. It might, I think, be just as accurate as an imitation of the bird's cry if written *pilldeer* or *tilldeer*. In parts of the West Indies the name is *tildeo*, a pretty word certainly and a good imitation of the cry.

Spotted Sandpiper

Actitis macularia

For many years the Sutton family's home was in northern West Virginia. Our white house perched on the highest part of a two-acre tract that sloped gently down to Buffalo Creek. The upper half of the tract was lawn, but the lower part, which was subject to mild flooding, was garden, and the vegetables grown there were the pride of the neighborhood. Had there been no garden, giant ragweed would have taken over, but my father saw to it that the ragweed never had a chance, so the creek's edge was "lovesome" with butterflies, shiny blue-green damselflies with black wings, an aquatic plant called frog's-bit or waterweed, and dainty little waders that the villagers called tilt-ups or teeter-snipes, Spotted Sandpipers.

We saw and heard the sandpipers daily from early spring to mid-fall, though I never found a nest on our place. They were especially noticeable in summer when the creek became a series of quiet pools connected by shallow riffles. Individuals that we saw were usually adults with heavily spotted underparts, but in late summer many were young birds with plain white underparts. Whatever their plumage, they were instantly recognizable in several ways. Their whistled *pee-tweet* was unmistakable. Their circling out from shore on widespread wings just above the water was unlike that of any other shorebird that I knew. But especially distinctive was the all but continuous tipping or bobbing of the hind end, a movement that looked as if more effort was put into pushing the tail down than in lifting it up. Watching that tail, I could not keep from mind an uncontrollable spell of hiccups. The tipping seemed as integral a part of the bird's physiology as walk-

49

ing or flying or breathing. I did occasionally, though not often, see a bird standing in the shade, with eyes half-closed and tail-end quiet, possibly napping.

I found many Spotted Sandpiper nests upstream from the village in 1915 and 1917. All were fairly close to water and partly hidden by low-growing vegetation. Since eggs were laid after the spring flooding as a rule, many of them won out over the predators and hatched. The downy chicks were white below and ashy gray above, with a dark line down the middle of the back. Just after hatching they were wonderfully delicate in appearance, but actually they were pretty tough. Once properly dried-out, they ran about nimbly, even swiftly, bobbing their hind ends just as vigorously as any adult ever did. I couldn't help indulging myself in a bit of hyperbole about that bobbing at so early an age. Did even an embryo about to hatch occasionally bob? The question did not seem altogether silly.

I was to see much of *Actitis macularia* in my wanderings later in life. I saw it in Hudson Bay along the east coast as far north as Richmond Gulf in 1926 and along the west coast at the mouth of the Churchill River in 1931. I learned that it had a remarkably wide altitudinal breeding range—from sea-level in many parts of North America and up to eleven or twelve thousand feet in the Rocky Mountain cordillera. It was truly adaptable, capable of living under a great variety of ecological conditions. One fact about it somehow impressed me more than others: in Mexico, in winter, it seemed to be just as much at home under the moss-hung cypresses and ceibas along the Rio Sabinas as it did under the sycamores and willows along Buffalo Creek.

The Spotted Sandpiper shares with certain other shore-birds the habit of alighting above ground on shrubbery, low trees, and wires when agitated by a human being's proximity to nest or chicks. No part of its aerial courtship display is at all spectacular. The performing bird rises slowly on rapidly beating wings, repeating its shrill *pee-tweet* as long as it moves upward. As for ground displays little has been published that makes clear what each sex

Spotted Sandpiper, *Actitis macularia*. Utah, 1962.
Velma Harris, F.P.S.A.

does. Courting birds deserve watching and more needs to be known about them. I cannot say when displays are most likely to take place. Spring after spring in West Virginia and Pennsylvania I watched for them without seeing more than an occasional chasing of one bird by another, as if the whole business of pairing had been settled on the wintering ground or during northward migration.

On May 4, 1958, however, at a small impoundment in central Oklahoma, I witnessed unforgettable strutting and posturing of at least one of four or five birds along a short stretch of shore. I collected no specimen, so do not know what the sex of the participants was. I saw very little chasing of one bird by another; there was no copulation; the occasional flights upward on quivering wings were not especially noticeable. Most of the action was on the ground. But the way in which one bird (or another) would stand with head high, chest puffed out, and partly spread wings held so that the tips pointed straight groundward was grotesque, even funny. The posture was repeated often enough to give me a clear impression. I even made a pencil sketch of it in my notebook—this from memory, not on the spot. Another posture required leaning far forward with head down, half-spread wings drooping, and partly fanned tail sticking straight up.

Upland Sandpiper

Bartramia longicauda

In a big strawberry patch just beyond the town limits of Eureka, north-central Illinois, a pair of Upland Sandpipers nested in the spring of 1910. When the birds first appeared that year they made their presence known by alighting on fenceposts along the edge of the patch, by circling on rapidly beating wings a hundred feet in air, and by giving a bubbly cry that sounded like *wheel-ily* to me. Occasionally the *wheel-ily* was prolonged into a descending whinny so remarkable that—even though I was not yet in my teens—I wondered how the birds' vocal apparatus could produce it. "We called them prairie whistlers when I was a boy," my father said. We knew they nested on the farm (in Ford County, northeastern Illinois), for they stayed all spring, but we never found a nest. The plovers that warmed on the freshly plowed fields were a bird of a different kind. His "plovers" were Lesser Golden-Plovers (*Pluvialis dominica*), a species that migrates northward regularly through the Mississippi valley.

Professor Compton at Eureka College showed me two stuffed specimens of the "strawberry-patch birds" that I asked him about. "The correct name for them is Upland Plover," he said. I watched the pair closely while I picked berries, being especially impressed by the way in which they held their full-spread wings high over their backs just after alighting. I did not find the nest, but someone else did, for picking the berries required attention to every row of plants. When I looked at the four eggs, I thought there was a mixup, for they seemed far too large for a bird the size of the two I had been watching. I asked Professor Compton to show me the specimens again. "When the

53

young ones hatch," the professor said, "they are so well developed that they start running around as soon as their down dries off. The eggs have to be big."

All four eggs probably hatched, but I never found the chicks or the empty shells. The parent birds probably saw to it that their brood stayed scattered and well away from us who were picking the berries.

When the Sutton family moved to Texas, I was to find that what everybody called the Field Plover was the very species I had seen in Illinois. I remembered the *wheel-ily* callnote well and was genuinely surprised by hearing it so often at night in late summer, and in early fall. All those night calls were from birds moving southward high in the sky. Some birds stopped on the prairie to feed, but I never saw a nesting pair.

I noticed that the *wheel-ily* notes in the sky seemed to come from birds that were widely scattered. I could not see them, of course, but no two calls heard at the same time ever seemed to come from the same place overhead. I decided that the birds were not in flocks. As I continued to observe the species I found that even in areas where many were feeding they did not go about in flocks.

That *wheel-ily* continued to be one of my favorite bird calls. During the past thirty years in Oklahoma I have heard it often, though I have observed only a few breeding pairs. A pair that Karl W. Haller and I happened upon in the northeastern corner of the state on June 12, 1937, had small chicks.

Nowadays the Upland Plover is called the Upland Sandpiper. In flat areas subject to flooding along Lake Texoma's north shore, I have often seen transient birds in late summer. There the young cocklebur plants have been just high and dense enough to hide the sandpipers completely as they fed. As I walked through the tough weeds the birds would flush one by one, never in a flock, calling as they flew off not far above ground. Instead of alighting they kept on, moving high into the sky and heading south. How many more times would they stop to feed and rest

Upland Sandpiper, *Bartramia longicauda*. Oklahoma, 1975.
John S. Shackford.

before reaching their winter home in Argentina? All of them flew well, but the body plumage of specimens that I collected was in heavy molt.

I continue to be puzzled about Upland Sandpipers that I hear and see in early July. Are they adult birds that have failed in their nesting and are moving southward before they really need to? Are they young birds of early broods? Eggs are said to have been seen or collected as late as June 13 in New England, June 11 in Pennsylvania, May 27 in New Jersey, June 15 and July 1 in "Saskatchewan, Manitoba, Dakotas, and Minnesota," and May 20 and June 17 in "Ohio to Iowa and Kansas" (A.C. Bent, 1929, *U.S. Natl. Mus. Bull.* 146, Pt. 2, p. 61). Eggs have been found in Oklahoma as late as June 1 in Washita County, June 12 in Oklahoma County, and June 24 in Cimarron County. Young hatched as late as this will obviously not be ready for migration during the first week in July. My guess is that birds hatched in Oklahoma start migrating in August and late July, molting all their juvenal feathers except the wing quills as they move southward.

Common Snipe

Gallinago gallinago

One of the most exciting experiences of my younger days was discovering, in northwestern Pennsylvania, a breeding population of Common Snipes. Known at the time as the Wilson's Snipe, the bird was believed to be a species different from the Common Snipe of the Old World. Allegedly it had sixteen tail feathers, whereas the Old World bird had fourteen usually, but sometimes twelve, sixteen, or eighteen.

The breeding population that I found inhabited Pymatuning Swamp, an extensive wilderness area of bogs, cattail marshes, tamaracks, hemlocks, poison sumac, pitcher plants, and showy lady's slippers. My headquarters were at the old Century Inn in the village of Hartstown. A big cattail marsh was just across the Pittsburgh and Lake Erie Railway tracks from the hotel. Two railway roadbeds crossed the swamp. When one of these sank too far into the bog, trains ran over the other. One roadbed or the other was always in a state of repair.

On that first evening in April, 1922, I heard the snipes hooting or bleating as they flew in wide circles over the cattails. The windy sound was delightful. It was quite new to me, for though I had seen many of the snipes in Texas, I had never heard them performing. When I waded around the following day, the snipes circled over me, sometimes so low that the sound of their hooting was a bit unsettling. I couldn't resist the feeling that they were trying to drive me off.

Presently, I found a nest with four eggs. These I collected, for I knew that the breeding record was important. The embryos in the eggs were well developed. The snipes

56

had, in other words, been there for some time. I counted several performing birds the following day without knowing whether they were males or females. Their hooting was especially loud in the morning and evening.

Since that early year I have seen much of *Gallinago gallinago* in the United States and Canada and in Iceland (whose population in the past has been more closely associated taxonomically with the Old World form). As I watched the birds performing above low-lying meadows between the city of Reykjavik and its airport, I looked hard for one feature—the outermost feather on each side of the spread tail. According to many drawings that I had seen of displaying birds, these two feathers stick out separately from the rest of the tail. Many observers believe that the weird hooting or bleating or winnowing that has been written about so much is caused by the vibration of these two feathers.

I cannot help being skeptical about this explanation of the windy sound. In Iceland I failed to see the two feathers, though I watched performing birds closely. In Canada and the United States I certainly have not seen the two feathers sticking out separately from the rest of the tail, and this fact leads me to say, first, that in the New World form (now considered a geographical race) the feathers may not be equipped with muscles making the extra-wide spreading possible and, second, that if the Old World form *can* spread the two feathers separately whereas the New World form cannot, the two forms may indeed be two species rather than one.

Both the Old World and the New World forms have ground displays in which the tail is spread to its widest, lifted, and twitched from side to side. Some careful observing needs to be done. The tail feathers of the New World form need to be counted, not an easy thing to do for the feathers are hard to separate. Most museum specimens have not been prepared with widespread tails, and counting the feathers may necessitate such rough handling that the tail comes apart. Anyone who is in a position to exam-

Common Snipe, *Gallinago gallinago*. Manitoba, Canada, 1983.
James M. Richards.

ine large numbers of snipes shot as game should make a
point of counting the rectrices and reporting on his find-
ings. In no freshly shot, unskinned specimen that I have
handled have I found the slightest evidence that the outermost rectrix on each side of the tail is ever spread so widely
as to stick out noticeably.

American Woodcock

Scolopax minor

While living with my grandparents as a boy in southern Minnesota, I found a woodcock's nest. The four eggs were in the middle of a little-used road through woods near the Blue Earth River. I'd surely have stepped on those eggs had not the incubating bird moved from them with wings partly spread, fallen on its side as if crippled, then suddenly become uncrippled and whirred off. I marked the

American Woodcock, *Scolopax minor*. Ontario, Canada, 1981.
James M. Richards.

spot with a stick and visited it many times. The protective coloration of the bird amazed me. Its eyes were wide open; it knew that I was towering above it; yet it stayed right where it was until I almost touched it.

On many occasions since then I have seen a woodcock on its nest, or flushed it from an alder swale where holes in the damp ground showed where it had been probing, or listened to the odd *peent* that it utters between courtship flights in early spring. But only twice have I had a clear look at a woodcock while it was moving about on the ground, feeding. So accustomed is the bird to its invisibility that it takes that invisibility for granted no matter where it is. On September 29, 1952, at a woodsy spot in central Oklahoma, several of us watched a woodcock probing in the mud close to a trickle flowing from an impounded spring. It behaved as if wholly unaware that anyone was watching it though we were only a few yards away. On November 9, 1952, two students and I watched one for about ten minutes as it walked farther and farther from cover on a mudflat bordering a pond near Holdenville, east-central Oklahoma. It obviously was finding something to eat, for we could see it swallowing worms that its long bill brought up.

The male woodcock's "sky-dance" in spring is worth going a long way to see. I have witnessed the performance many times in northwestern Pennsylvania, where, between a small lake and a tamarack bog, there was a dry stretch across which a dirt road ran. A favorite courting ground was just south of this road, so I could hear the *peent* of several widely scattered males if I walked far enough along it. One male's spot was only a few yards from the road. Ensconcing myself near this spot, I waited for night to shut down. About the time everything but the sky had become vague and almost colorless, I'd hear the oddly squeezed-out *peent* only a few rods off, and I'd wonder how the bird had got there without my seeing him. Thus, *peent* after *peent*, he sounded off for ten minutes or so. Then, after a long pause, I heard the musical wing-whir of the rising bird and *saw* him as he flew above the road perhaps thirty feet in air. He was not clearly visible, but I could see him well enough to tell that he was moving rapidly upward. The wing-whirring continued for several seconds, then stopped and the sky-dance started. He was well above the ground by this time, and quite out of sight, but his twittering told me about where he was, and I listened, enthralled. There was something so out-of-character about the sound! Could that essentially terrestrial bird actually be making it, up there between me and the faint stars? It sounded like the excited chirping of some canary-sized bird pitching itself recklessly about, heedless of any such thing as collision. When the twittering stopped, I listened hard, hoping to hear the whisper of return to earth, but could hear nothing, absolutely nothing, until off beyond the roadside weeds the buzzed-out *peent* started again.

The twittering usually continues until the bird has reached the ground. Could my presence at the roadside have caused the bird's silence as it descended?

The woodcock has been seen on many occasions in summer west of its long-known breeding grounds in eastern Oklahoma, but many of us have thought that these midsummer birds were early migrants moving leisurely southward or non-breeding individuals wandering about in search of damp ground in which to probe. On April 5, 1973, however, John S. Barclay and his students observed a displaying male near Lake Carl Blackwell, north-central Oklahoma, and two days later they caught and banded a chick there—proof at last of breeding in a habitat that had always been considered too dry for woodcocks. Then, on March 31, 1974, William A. Carter caught and banded three chicks on his place near Ada, east-central Oklahoma, again in country that had been thought not right for a woodcock's breeding. Thus has it come to pass that midsummer sightings in central Oklahoma are believed to be evidence of widespread breeding in that part of the state.

Scolopax minor has never, so far as I know, been seen in the Oklahoma Panhandle, but there are many records for the main body of the state. Finding the courting males may not be easy, for the spots they choose may be in thickets that human beings do not often visit in late winter. Bear in mind that William A. Carter found that brood of young on the last day of March. Incubation requires about twenty days. Laying three or four eggs requires at least one day per egg. So courtship displaying must have been going on near Ada in very early March or late February! How I wish I'd been there to witness it!

Mourning Dove

Zenaida macroura

People are pretty well informed about birds today, young and old alike, yet every spring someone is sure to ask "What kind of owl is it that we've been hearing recently?" I do my best at imitating the Mourning Dove's mellifluous *oo-oooo-oo oo, oo, oo*, a song I've known all my life, and watch the expression on the face of my interrogator change. "You mean to say that bird's a dove? You're sure it isn't an owl?"

When I hear the familiar call near my house I know that one of "my" doves has returned. And I wonder where it has wintered. In Mexico perhaps? A dove banded as a nestling by Paul F. Nighswonger near Alva, Oklahoma, on July 20, 1952, was recovered in Jalisco, southwestern Mexico, in December of 1958. In southwestern Oklahoma per-

Mourning Dove, *Zenaida macroura*. Arizona, 1983.
Howard L. Kessler.

haps? In late January of 1966, almost four hundred doves were found dead from starvation in shelter belts, barns, and deserted buildings there. Winter is usually not bad in that part of the state.

In Norman, Oklahoma, the population of breeding doves fluctuates greatly, but during the past thirty years it has not been obviously cyclic. When there are many pairs in residential parts of the city one pair always nests in my yard. My pair's nests are in an old cedar of Lebanon. When I know the birds have returned, I listen for the first three syllables of the song. If the song stops there, if the final three syllables are missing, I know a nest is on its way.

In the summer of 1964, several pairs raised brood after brood on the university campus and one pair nested in my yard. My pair succeeded in bringing at least two broods off, but I'm not sure that the young doves survived. The nests disintegrated or became overcrowded, and down the chicks went before their time. I saw them side by side on the ground. They were well-feathered and looked healthy, but I fear the cats got them before they learned to fly. One campus pair used the same nest at least three times that summer. The nest was on a windowsill in a spot the wind seldom reached.

The literature dealing with the Mourning Dove's biology makes clear that the female selects the nest site and stays there, letting her mate bring the twigs, pieces of dead weed, etc., for the nest. An excellent photograph has been taken of the female crouched on the partly finished nest with the male, twig in beak, standing on her back. According to my observations, such behavior is exceptional. What I have seen has, as a rule, been one bird busily searching for twigs on the ground, seizing one, and fluttering up to a partly built nest where, without help from a mate, it has added the bit to the flimsy structure. Nest-building behavior is characteristic. On the ground the dove moves rapidly, looking this way and that, obviously eager to find material that will do. It is not very choosy; once it has picked up a twig or pine needle it does not look for more but flies directly to the nest, at which no mate is waiting. Campus doves are so used to the passing students that they do not seem to mind being watched. Never have I seen a Mourning Dove breaking a twig from a dead branch as the domestic pigeons sometimes do when nest-building.

At a campus nest I banded what might have been a second brood for the season on April 18, 1964. The nest was in a small pine only eleven feet up, so it was easy to watch and climb to. At that same nest I watched one of the parent doves feeding another almost fledged brood a month later (May 20). To my great surprise the parent, after making clear to its young that no further food was to be pumped up for them, flew to the ground, walked rapidly about, picked up a twig, and flew to a half-finished nest well up in an elm about thirty yards away. No mate was waiting for it there. It added the twig to the nest and flew off.

In central Oklahoma most dove nests are in trees, but on the High Plains at the west end of the Panhandle many pairs nest on or close to the ground in the sand-sage. It strikes me as remarkable that the young survive, for coyotes are common in that country. On a ranch five miles northeast of Guymon I have found many doves nesting, year after year, near a marshy spot among Russian olives and sapling willows. Nests there have been only a few yards apart, some on the ground, some a few feet up. A special study should be made of that spot.

One spring I flushed a dove from its nest (two eggs) about ten feet up in a tree near a path along the east edge of Norman. I hid myself close by, interested in learning whether one or both birds of the pair would return to the nest. Presently, a Blue Jay (*Cyanocitta cristata*) flew over, looked down, saw the two white eggs, suddenly wheeled, alighted near the nest, and hopped to it. Two jabs of the jay's bill, each followed by a lifting of the crested head, and the eggs were no longer there. I found the shells on the ground under the nest.

Yellow-billed Cuckoo

Coccyzus americanus

A creature of mystery called the rain crow was an important part of my early boyhood in Nebraska and Minnesota. I often heard it but never saw it. Presumably it was black. Its call was a rapidly repeated *kuck* or *kluck* followed by a slowed-down series of *kelps* or *kowks* that emanated not from any particular tree but from somewhere off in the woods or orchard. "When you hear one of those rain crows," the neighbors said, "it's going to rain." And it often did.

My one bird book, Chapman's *Bird-Life*, had not a word to say about rain crows, but it did have a colored picture of a Yellow-billed Cuckoo and when, as a ten-year-old in Illinois, I found a dead yellow-bill on the campus of Eureka College, Professor Compton straightened things out for me when he said, "People call that bird the rain crow because they hear it just before a storm. It calls in all sorts of weather, but no one seems to hear it unless a storm's coming."

I was to learn that the best way to see Yellow-billed Cuckoos was to visit trees whose foliage was being devoured by webworms. The slender, long-tailed birds had a way of slipping in and out by a leafy route and they hopped from branch to branch often without spreading their wings. While watching for the yellow-bill, I became acquainted with its cousin, the Black-billed Cuckoo (*C. erythropthalmus*), a less common species whose outer tail feathers were much less noticeably tipped with white, whose wings were without a rufous tinge, and whose eyes were surrounded with a featherless area of red skin. The call notes of the two species were so much alike that they

66

Yellow-billed Cuckoo, *Coccyzus americanus*, nestling.
Kansas, 1962. Orville O. Rice.

sounded like imitations of each other; and they included a gentle, almost musical *coo-coo* or *coo-coo-coo* that had a delightful faraway quality.

Then I began finding nests, all of them—of both species—flat, rather poorly constructed of twigs, and lined with dry catkins and leaf skeletons rather than feathers or hair. The eggs were pale blue, those of the black-bill being a bit smaller and slightly more greenish than those of the yellow-bill. What surprised me most about the nests was their lowness: not one of them was over ten feet above the ground. The birds themselves always seemed to be in the trees well above me, but the nests were so low that I could see or feel into them without having to climb much, if at all.

Shortly after finding my first cuckoo nests, I read of the famed cuckoo of Europe, the bird that built no nest of its own, laid its eggs in the nest of smaller birds, and let these small "host" species raise the young cuckoos. In what I read appeared the statement that our New World yellow-bills and black-bills sometimes laid their eggs in each other's nests. So I paid close attention to what I found in every cuckoo nest, hoping that I might add a bit to what the world knew about social parasitism among birds.

I found no egg in any cuckoo nest that did not, so far as I could tell, belong there. What I did find was newly hatched chicks that were the most unbirdlike creatures I had ever seen. They were dark-skinned and covered with grayish white "hairs" that looked as if they'd been smeared on, and their mouth lining was so bizarre that when I first saw it I feared some dread disease had attacked the brood. So hungry were the nestlings that they tried to swallow my finger. As they grew older those natal "hairs" were pushed out by the burgeoning blood-quills, whose spiny appearance made the chicks look like small, strangely-shaped hedgehogs. There were times when I seriously wondered what was happening to those young cuckoos. Were the little things drying up like flower buds deprived of moisture? Had they not had such voracious appetites, I'd have considered them done-for. Came the day when the blood-quills feathered out and lo, the nestlings were real cuckoos after all. And they were pretty, though comically stub-tailed.

Someone may have photographed in color the open mouths of nestling yellow-bills and black-bills. I suspect that there is a difference between the two species in this part of their anatomy, but I do not know what that difference is. A photograph of a young yellow-bill begging for food shows the mouth-lining to be red. I suspect that the black-bill's mouth lining is equally bright, but yellow or orange rather than red. Work remains to be done on this. I also wonder whether the dark upperparts of a young yellow-bill ever have the scaly appearance that young black-bills have there as a result of the light gray feather edgings. No nestling yellow-bill that I have seen had very bright eyelids. The area around the eye in the young black-bill is yellow. I wonder when the yellow of that area changes to red—perhaps about the time the bird is ready to leave for its winter home south of the United States?

Greater Roadrunner

Geococcyx californianus

Most people do not really know the roadrunner. They have heard wild tales about the way in which it surrounds a rattler with cactus pads and makes the snake so angry that it thrashes about, getting itself full of spines, and dies. They have heard tales less wild, about men who have tried in vain, afoot or on horseback, to match a roadrunner's speed. They have seen cartoons. Chaparral or chaparral-cock is what they have called the uncouth, ground-inhabiting cuckoo.

He who really knows the roadrunner has watched it on a cool spring morning, moving from branch to branch to the top of a dead tree, there to perch with wings spread, tail down, and plumage opened up to let the warmth of the rising sun reach the featherless areas on its back. Or flushing a big grasshopper into flight and capturing the insect with a graceful leap into the air. Or moving slowly across a rocky slope on its way to a nestful of young with a big lizard in its bill. Or singing its dovelike song with head held high at the first of the coos, then lower and lower with each coo until—as one cowboy reported the action—"its beak is laying on the rock" at the very end.

Much of what has been written about the roadrunner gives it an aura of wildness, yet repeatedly I have observed a roadrunner hanging around camp looking for a handout or following a railroad right-of-way into town, catching grasshoppers. Here in Norman the species has nested within city limits. One nest was about four feet up in a juniper at the corner of an unoccupied house. No one would have known the nest was there had neighbors not seen the birds carrying mice across the yard, onto the front

70

steps, and into the juniper. At another house a roadrunner frequented the premises all summer and delighted everyone by finding a nook in which to roost just above a first-floor window. Crowded into its sleeping quarters, with tail sticking straight up against the wall, it looked serenely down at those who had come to watch it.

A nestful of young roadrunners is a sight to see. Just hatched, they resemble reptiles covered with grayish white hairs.

Greater Roadrunner, *Geococcyx californianus*. Texas, 1976. Kathleen G. Beal.

If hungry, they open their oddly marked mouths and emit a hoarse little bellow, begging for food. If one of the brood has recently been fed, the tail of a lizard protrudes from the not-quite-shut bill and the baby has the good grace not to beg for more. If the brood is nearly fledged they do no begging. Instead, they leap from the nest and do their best to get away, but they are too weak to go far. Some petting and talking-to convince them that they should "stay put" a while longer.

Famed for its snake killing—the roadrunner actually does catch snakes up to two feet or so long—it is also preyed upon by snakes. In Custer County, Oklahoma, on August 1, 1955, Otis M. King found a nest with eight young, two considerably larger than the others. The following day there were only five young (the two largest probably had fledged) and a sixth was inside a large coachwhip snake only two feet away. On August 3, the nest held five young, two of them vigorous, two small and weak, one emaciated and dead. The nest was five and a half feet up in a small mulberry not far from the town of Weatherford.

Of the many roadrunner nests that I have found, only one held eight eggs. The whole clutch had, I believe, been laid by one female bird. At the nest discussed above, two females might have laid the eggs. The cuckoos of the world are notably irregular in their breeding behavior. I see no reason why the roadrunner should be orthodox in its nesting when it is unorthodox in so many other ways.

The roadrunner inhabits all of Oklahoma. I have seen more of it in the Black Mesa country than elsewhere in the state, but it is locally common in many areas. Oklahoma, southern Kansas, Arkansas, and southwestern Missouri are along the north edge of its range. Since the bird is almost flightless and strictly nonmigratory, it does not always survive winter weather in this part of the world.

For years I have entertained the idea that roadrunners might hole up, even hibernate, when winter weather turns really bad. The winter of 1978–79 was severe in central Oklahoma. What I learned of the roadrunner's activities that winter convinced me that a combination of snow, cold, and wind can kill roadrunners outright, despite their being able to catch small birds and find shelter out of the wind. Roadrunners are not warmly clothed. Much of their body heat must be lost through their long legs and the bare space around and back of the eye. Reports that reached me in the winter of 1978–79 made clear that the birds were not doing well. At a house east of Norman one bird spent much time on a porch, as if glad to have found a place without snow. At a garage, a roadrunner hung around waiting for the return of a car under which it could warm up. Oddly enough, no one found a roadrunner dead anywhere, but one bird that was brought to me was badly emaciated and almost done for.

The behavior of roadrunners in winter at this northern edge of range deserves careful study. The stomach contents of every specimen collected or found dead in winter should be carefully identified.

Common Barn-Owl

Tyto alba

Forget, if you can, the barn-owl's somewhat uncouth appearance, its solemn facial expression, and its way of standing there with wings slouchily folded, heels knocking against each other but feet well apart, looking for all the world like a comedian who expects to bring the house down with his loose-hung, half apologetic stance without making a move or saying a word. Forget all this, and you may find yourself considering the barn-owl among the most beautiful of birds. The plumage of its underparts has the softness and luster of fine silken fabrics, and the grays, browns, and buffs of its upperparts are so wonderfully harmonious that they rouse the admiration, if not the awe, of the beholder.

The species has been in existence a long while. Fossil remains of *Tyto alba* dating back to the Pleistocene have been found in Florida and California. It ranges widely today, being found on all the continents, though nowhere in polar areas and not, oddly enough, in Hawaii or New Zealand, where so many non-endemic birds have thrived after being introduced there by mankind. Strong winds and the barn-owl's disproportionately great wingspread may have helped it in its conquest of the world.

In Oklahoma the Common Barn-Owl is found not in heavily wooded areas inhabited by the more powerful Great Horned Owl (*Bubo virginianus*) and Barred Owl (*Strix varia*), but rather in rough, comparatively treeless grasslands throughout which there are many caves and sinkholes. In these underground recesses the barn-owls nest. The species' breeding season is long, starting in late February (nest with five eggs, one or more of which had been

73

Common Barn-Owl, *Tyto alba*. Ohio, 1973. Karl H. Maslowski.

laid in February, Craig County, northeastern Oklahoma, March 4) and lasting until October 1 (nest with several eggs, Payne County, north-central Oklahoma, a third clutch for the season and eggs did not hatch).

In Norman, central Oklahoma, I have seen the Common Barn-Owl only infrequently. Shortly after I started teaching at the university, I was called to the Administration Building to see "a queer bird" that was half asleep on a fire escape just outside a third-floor window. Had I been able to raise that window, I might have caught the owl in my hands. On another occasion jays screamed "Owl!" so loudly near the Ellison Infirmary that I had to go for a look. There, sure enough, perched a barn-owl, half hidden by the elm's leafage, about fifteen feet from the ground.

But the experience that is clearest in my memory was with two Common Barn-Owls that I believe were courting. The date was April 5, 1962. That evening I had attended a function at the Student Union and was making my way homeward across the campus between ten and eleven o'clock. Suddenly my attention was roused by a strange, rather loud double-clicking that seemed to echo among the buildings. I guessed that the sound was produced by a large katydid and surmised that the insect's position on a windowsill or high wall was responsible for the amplification of its pronouncements. Then I realized that students were cutting sentences short, stopping in their tracks, and gazing skyward. I, too, looked up, and there, about two hundred feet above us, clearly visible since the white of their underparts reflected the lights below them, were two Common Barn-Owls. They were flying in narrow circles, following each other closely. Even as we watched, one of them gave a harsh scream. Beating their great wings gracefully, double-clicking (perhaps, though not certainly, with their mandibles), and screaming occasionally, the eerie twosome drifted northwestward beyond the sphere of light and disappeared. Whether they were a male and female or rival individuals of the same sex, and whether both did the double-clicking and screaming, I shall never know. I do suspect, however, that courtship was going on and I wonder if the lights of the campus had attracted the birds. So far as I know, the Common Barn-Owl has never nested on or near the campus.

One thought crosses my mind: If the pair bond is strong, if pairs remain faithful to each other year after year, then perhaps not much courtship display takes place. In the considerable literature at hand about *Tyto alba*, I find next to nothing about its courtship.

Screech-Owl

Otus asio

Among the loveliest night sounds of the winter woods are the quavering whistle and velvet-smooth trill of this little owl. The calls must be important in fall and early winter—the time of courtship and pairing—for even a clumsy imitation of them at those seasons will sometimes draw the owl close. How exciting it is to have the beautiful creature, all big golden eyes, looking hard in your direction *for that other owl!*

Throughout much of its wide range, *Otus asio* is so common in towns that it is almost a dooryard bird. It does not, as a rule, live in "big timber" inhabited by the Great Horned Owl and Barred Owl, much larger species that feed on Screech-Owls, presumably when other prey is scarce. On a Thanksgiving day in West Virginia years ago, a neighbor who had shot a Barred Owl gave me the specimen. After skinning and mounting it, I examined the contents of its stomach. The many feathers there, washed and dried, proved to be those of a Screech-Owl.

In eastern North America, *Otus asio* comes in two color-phases, a red (reddish brown) and a gray. The plumage patterns of the two phases differ strikingly, those of gray birds being far the more intricate on the underparts. Differences of color and pattern are independent of sex, age, or season, and they are absolute—gray birds stay gray, red ones red. The differences between red and gray birds are so great that I cannot help wondering how it has come about that the two phases co-exist side by side today. We have been led to believe that whatever exists represents a "survival of the fittest," yet here is a species whose dichromatism declares that red birds are just as "fit" as gray

76

ones or, what is even more puzzling, that existence of the species *may depend upon a continuance of the two phases.*

What I have found in Oklahoma is thought-provoking. Throughout most of the state *Otus asio* is two-phased, but west of the 100th meridian the red phase virtually disappears. A specimen from Texas County in the Panhandle is partly gray, partly red. In the Black Mesa Country still farther west every bird is gray. Grayness characterizes most Screech-Owls from the western edge of the Great Plains westward to the Pacific Ocean. Birds of the Rocky Mountain cordillera are all gray.

Screech-Owls of Oklahoma's Black Mesa country differ from those of the main body of the state in that they have no quavering whistle. They quickly respond to an imitation of the eastern bird's purred trill, but I am not sure that the trill is one of their own calls. Black Mesa birds are surprisingly common among the big trees along the Cimarron River and its major tributaries. Great Horned Owls inhabit the same area, but I suspect that small mammals are so abundant there that the big owls only rarely capture Screech-Owls.

I am plotting in detail the distribution of the Screech-Owl's color phases as they exist in Oklahoma today. A hundred years from now it will be interesting to see whether the red phase has completely disappeared from the Panhandle, whether some birds along the 100th meridian are of mixed phase, etc. At this writing I believe that where the habitat is strongly "western"—that is semi-arid, subject to violent weather changes, and thinly wooded—the red phase does not survive. Inevitably a suspicion lingers that gray birds of the Rocky Mountains (and of the Black Mesa country) are of a different species from the two-phased form of the main body of the state.*

*The most recent edition of *Check-list of North American Birds* (1983, American Ornithologists' Union) was published after this account was completed. The *Check-list* now recognizes as different species the Eastern Screech-Owl (*Otus asio*) and the Western Screech-Owl (*O. kennicottii*).

Eastern Screech-Owl, *Otus asio*, red color phase. Florida (?), 1969. Allan D. Cruickshank/VIREO.

Eastern Screech-Owl, *Otus asio*, gray color phase. Ontario, Canada, 1974. James M. Richards.

In their thirty-year study of the Screech-Owls of northern Ohio, Laurel F. VanCamp and Charles J. Henny (1975, U.S. Dept. Interior, Fish & Wildlife Service, North American Fauna No. 71, pp. 43–47, 61) found that, during the extremely cold and snowy December of 1951, mortality was higher among red birds than gray, and that between 1951 and 1975 the red birds did not regain their pre-1951 abundance. Is it possible that the colors and patterns of red birds drain-off body heat more rapidly than those of gray birds, or that red birds are caught more frequently by predators than gray ones simply because they are more visible? James A. Mosher and Charles J. Henny (1976, Auk 93: 614–19) found that at low temperatures there was a "significant difference in oxygen uptake" in birds of the two phases, a difference great enough, it would seem, to kill off the red birds in really bad weather. After the extremely cold December of 1951, the red phase fell from 23.3 percent of the Screech-Owl population to 14.7 percent in Ohio, a drop suggesting that the gray birds are better fitted than the red for surviving periods of extreme environmental stress.

Great Horned Owl

Bubo virginianus

A remarkably hardy creature, the Great Horned Owl starts nesting—even in the northern United States and Canada—long before winter ends. I have seen many an incubating bird with its back covered with snow. In the southern Great Plains, eggs are often laid in February, less often in January. Nesting early evidently works out well, for the species ranges throughout wooded parts of the continental New World northward almost to tree-limit and southward to southern South America, and in many areas it is common. It is warmly feathered. Food in the form of rabbits, squirrels, and birds is obtainable no matter how cold the air or deep the snow.

The great horn is wonderfully adaptable. Even in small patches of woods and in park-like areas in towns it finds a home. It does not build its own nest. If no old hawk, crow, or squirrel nest is available to it, it lays its eggs in a hollow stub, on a cliff ledge, in a deserted building, or at the forking of the trunk of a large tree. The white eggs are conspicuous, but they are not often left uncovered once incubation starts.

Whether or not pairs mate for life, some courtship hooting goes on in the fall, long before egg-laying starts. The female, being the larger of the pair, has the deeper voice. If the pair has raised a normally early first brood, the young ones are obtaining at least some of their own food before the summer's end. If, on the other hand, brood-rearing has been delayed by destruction of the first clutch of eggs, the second clutch may not be laid until April or May and the old birds may have to provide food for the chicks all summer long. A pair that I observed from Au-

Great Horned Owl, *Bubo virginianus*. New Mexico, 1984.
Dale A. and Marian A. Zimmerman.

gust 14 to October 24, 1949, in Michigan must have lost their first clutch or very young chicks to raccoons (*Procyon lotor*) or other predators, and the female went ahead with a second clutch. The young of the late brood I continued to hear almost daily in August. Their cry was a wheezy whine with considerable carrying power. By October 22 the hooting of the old birds was noticeable by day as well as at night. The peevish cries of the chicks continued. At about sunset on October 24, as I was listening to the old birds, which were about half a mile apart, and to the young ones, both fairly near me, the nearer young one suddenly flew toward an old apple tree in which the male parent was perching. As the chick alighted there was a cacophony of hooting, whimpering, and loud bill-popping, the last from both birds. As the rumpus ended, the chick fell forward until, with feet clutching a branch and wings beating wildly, it hung head downward. The parent lifted his tail, hooted loudly, and flew off, even as the chick righted itself and also flew off—but not in the same direction. The old bird now surprised me by flying back to the top of a telephone pole near me where, with tail up, he hooted loudly. Never have I seen an adult great horn behave as that male did. I believe he was beside himself with annoyance.

Great horns are not active at the nest while eggs are being incubated. During this quiet period, other birds of prey whose nesting starts later than that of the owls, sometimes nest close by. A low great horn nest that I found in central Oklahoma on March 28, 1959, was almost under a Red-tailed Hawk's nest that the hawks may not have started to use until after the owl's eggs had been laid. The two nests were in the same big tree, the owl's about fifteen feet up, the hawks' about seventy feet up. Would that I knew how many young those two nests produced!

The lowest great horn nest I have ever seen was in an old White-necked Raven's (*Corvus cryptoleucus*) nest in the yard of a deserted farmhouse in the Oklahoma Panhandle. It held three half-grown owls. Standing on the ground just below them, I could stroke their feathered feet. This did not seem to annoy them, for they did not even pop their beaks at me. One of the parent birds I saw flying in the distance. I was glad it did not attack, for a great horn's talons and beak are powerful.

I have wondered why the great horn's clutch-size is so small. Most nests have two eggs, some only one, some three, a very few, four. Three young are often successfully reared. When prey (including insects, slugs, and crayfish) is abundant in summer the parent owls have no difficulty keeping their broods and themselves alive; but by fledging time some prey species have become rare or difficult to obtain, and when the young birds are obliged to obtain their own food in fall, they may have a hard time as winter approaches *unless all are in tip-top condition*. That, I believe, is the crux of the matter and probably the reason for the species' traditional adherence to the two-eggs per clutch rule: if two young only are reared, both are of just the right weight, both are able to capture their own food, and both stand a good chance of surviving.

Snowy Owl

Nyctea scandiaca

On May 25, 1930, on Southampton Island at the north end of Hudson Bay, I found my first Snowy Owl's nest. It was in the very heart of a drift of old snow and its six eggs lay in an inch of icy water. I'd never have found it had not the owl flown from it as I was walking past. To my surprise the big bird did not attack me. Instead it alighted some distance away, fell forward until lying flat, shook its wings without lifting or spreading them, and whined feebly, as if sick or disabled. Needing the eggs for the Carnegie Museum's collection, I took them back to the trading post and prepared them as specimens. Had I known what I know now, I'd not have taken them. The clutch was probably incomplete. Had I let the owl complete her clutch I might have undertaken a study of incubation, hatching procedure, and brood development. Eggs are laid about forty-eight hours apart and incubation begins with the laying of the first egg.

In the summer of 1953, at the head of Frobisher Bay on Baffin Island, David F. Parmelee and I had a wonderful time studying the breeding behavior of the owls, for several pairs nested within twenty miles of our base. We did a lot of walking that summer. The season was advanced by the time we had located all the nests. Each contained well-incubated eggs or chicks of assorted sizes, the newly hatched ones pure white, the larger ones more or less slaty gray. At some nests the oldest chick stood a foot or so high, while the youngest was only a little larger than the egg in which it had spent the first thirty to thirty-five days of its life.

We saw no injury-feigning among the parent owls on Baffin Island. Instead, they attacked, and we were obliged

Snowy Owl, *Nyctea scandiaca*. Oklahoma, 1975. John S. Shackford.

to protect ourselves. Had they hit us in the face they could have hurt us badly. I became convinced, as the summer passed, that attacking birds knew full well that we could not see them when they were directly between us and the brilliant sun. They had a way of hovering at that important point just before lunging at us.

One of my clearest memories of the latter part of that summer is of young birds that could fly well and probably were catching their own prey but were still partly covered with gray down that hung on them like a shaggy blanket.

Lemmings were plentiful that season, and the owls lived almost exclusively on them. At no nest that Dave and I visited did we find masses of decomposing lemmings like those that have been found around nestfuls of chicks in northern Alaska. Lemming populations are known to work up to a peak of abundance about every four years. The peak is followed by a "low," during which there are very few lemmings throughout vast areas. If the owls have become common as a result of having plenty of lemmings to eat and they find themselves without food, because the lemmings are no more, they have to move in order to find food and the move sometimes takes them southward far beyond the tundra. Wandering owls in search of food tend to invade treeless areas. If they find enough to eat in Canada's prairie provinces, they spend the winter there, but many move farther south, into the United States.

A question that deserves an answer is this: Do the birds that move far southward in winter ever go back to the breeding ground the following spring? Many owls that move into areas throughout which they are seldom seen are shot, but some survive. Do these survivors return to the Arctic, or has the food shortage that sent them south so weakened them that it has robbed them of the urge to return to the tundra?

So far as I know, no Snowy Owl banded in the far north and recovered during winter well south of the Arctic has ever been recovered again in the far north, nor has an owl banded well south of the Arctic ever been recovered in the Arctic. Every Snowy Owl that visits the southern Great Plains should, if possible, be banded on the chance that recovery will bring to light important facts. Catching the owls may not be easy, but live cotton rats (*Sigmodon hispidus*) should be good bait.

Common Nighthawk

Chordeiles minor

As kids we called them bullbats. And I recall the mixed feelings I had when told that "bullbat" was wrong and "nighthawk" right, for I knew that the long-winged birds were not true hawks and I knew that we all saw and heard them frequently in the daytime. To be sure, we saw them in the evening too. But when, in late summer and early fall, they were especially common, we saw them circling overhead at all hours in loose flocks, catching insects while on their way to their winter home. When migrating southward they never boomed. The booming was a midsummer performance.

As my study of Common Nighthawks intensified, I learned that there were "wild" populations of the birds as well as "tame" ones. To see the wild birds I had to go to the country, not to the woods but to rocky fields or open pasturelands, where the birds laid their two heavily spotted eggs in any sort of place, usually without the slightest attempt to hide them under vegetation. The "tame" birds nested on flat roofs—even in the heart of large cities. Many rooftop "nests" were in gravel, but one that I visited daily while drawing the incubating bird in watercolor was on tar paper. How the bird decided where to lay her eggs in the midst of that hot, uninviting expanse it would be hard to say. I did note that a crack and bit of sand kept the eggs from rolling around while the bird was not on them.

The Common Nighthawk has never nested, so far as I know, on any flat-roofed building in Norman, Oklahoma, but in late summer and fall it is a familiar visitor to residential parts of the city. People who have partly dead Chinese elms in their yards often call my attention to the "strange

Common Nighthawk, *Chordeiles minor*. Oklahoma, 1972.
E. Wayne Easley.

birds" that perch lengthwise on certain leafless branches.
These transients spend much of the day resting, start flying about after insects in the evening, and frequently break
a wing flying into wires. Not a fall has passed since my
coming to Norman in 1952 without someone's bringing to
me one or more of these badly crippled birds.

Toward the end of the southward migration, the Common Nighthawks that we see in town move about well
after dark, catching insects that swarm around the street
lights. Not one of these late transients has been brought to
me crippled. This may well be because the wires are visible
to the birds while they are flying close to the lights.

One summer we had a large breeding population of
nighthawks in a 160-acre tract near the Norman airport.
The area had been paved some time ago, but the pavement
was old, falling to pieces, and upgrown with weeds, strag-
gly grass, and salt-cedar. The nest-sites were scattered
widely, no two of them being at all close together. Egg-

laying probably started at about the same time for the several pairs of birds, but some eggs were destroyed and second clutches laid, so W. Marvin Davis, who marked and visited the nest-sites in his study of eighteen nestings, had every stage of development, from freshly-laid eggs to almost-fledged chicks, under surveillance at the height of the breeding season.

The chicks are delightful. When very young they pay little attention to those who stand over them; but when they become sparrow-size and their wing quills are feathering out, they have a most amusing way of opening their big mouths and hissing while at the same time spreading wide those utterly useless wings and running slowly off in a straight line like an ancient galleon under full sail.

There are facts about Common Nighthawks that deserve study. The species is a true caprimulgid, a member of the goatsucker family. It has a tiny bill, huge mouth, and large eyes. But the "shining carpet" layer of the choroid in those eyes has no fiery brilliance like that in the eyes of the Chuck-will's-widow, Whip-poor-will, and Common Poor-will. A flashlight directed toward a nighthawk at night gets only a dull glow from the eyes in response. What purpose, if any, does the brightness of the "shining carpet" serve? And what about the fact that nighthawks have no rictal bristles, those long, hair-like feathers that line the mouth?

Common Poorwill

Phalaenoptilus nuttallii

The poorwill may well be unique among birds in that it has been observed to hibernate. Certain swifts and humming-birds become torpid at times, entering a state that resembles hibernation; but a poorwill that was studied during three successive winters in the Colorado Desert area of Califor-nia was really hibernating. Those who studied it found it in the same niche in the rocks winter after winter. It had an astoundingly low body temperature (about 65° F.) and ex-ceedingly low rate of heartbeat, and its breathing was so imperceptible that no moisture collected on a "cold mirror . . . held directly in front of the nostrils" (Jaeger, 1949, *Condor*, 51:105–109). The tenacity the observers exhibited in visiting the bird's hibernating niche, in finding the bird winter after winter, and in ascertaining facts about it ap-peals to me as being among the truly remarkable biological odysseys of our time. That bird was not continuously im-mobile. If the weather became agreeable it would "come to" and fly about looking for food. But when it became truly torpid it could not (or at least would not) fold a wing that had been spread out by the person handling it.

The Common Poorwill is an Oklahoma bird. In the Black Mesa country at the west end of the Panhandle, it is fairly common in summer. It breeds eastward as far as Caddo County in southwestern Oklahoma, where Richard R. Graber and his wife, Jean, found a nest (two eggs) among junipers and small oaks in rough country near the village of Cogar on July 9, 1954. At that nest there were an egg and a chick on July 22 and two chicks on July 24. A female Common Poorwill collected in Pontotoc County, south-central Oklahoma, on July 5, 1967, almost certainly was breeding (W.A. Carter, 1968, *Bull. Oklahoma Ornithol. Soc.*, 1:19). Common Poorwills have been heard calling in spring and summer as far east as Osage and Washington counties in northeastern Oklahoma and as far as Murray County (Arbuckle Mountains) in south-central Oklahoma. All of which suggests that the species may breed widely in the state.

Where do Oklahoma's poorwills go in winter? Do some of them stay in one area all year, each finding a "niche in the rocks" if the weather turns bad? Guessing is pointless. Let me discuss what is known. On August 31, 1963, John S. Shackford and I flushed a single bird on a rocky slope in the Black Mesa country. John B. Semple and I saw and heard the species in the same area between September 20 and 26 in 1933. I have no further fall records for Cimarron County, this despite the fact that competent observers have visited that part of the state frequently in fall and winter during the past thirty years.

There are two other fall records for the Panhandle, each of a female found dead by Lawrence E. Dunn near Gate, Beaver County, in 1957, one on October 12, the other on October 24. The species probably nests in the hilly country along the Cimarron River north of Gate.

For the main body of the state there are many fall records, most of them for areas in which the Common Poorwill has not been found breeding. Near Alva, Woods County, Paul F. Nighswonger saw five or six active birds along a road on October 7 and 8, 1976, and two birds in the same area ten days later. The weather had "turned cold" thereabouts on October 16, but no snow had fallen. For the state's southwestern corner there are three records: one of three birds seen near Eldorado, Jackson County, on October 9, 1976 (Jack D. Tyler, John W. Ault III); another of one seen near Olustee, Jackson County, the following day (S.A. Krazovetz); another of one seen near Reed, Greer County, on October 2, 1976 (Joseph A. Grzybowski, Charles C. Carpenter). For the Wichita Mountains National Wildlife Refuge in Comanche County there are several records: one of six living birds seen and one in postjuvenal molt found dead on September 13, 1953 (W.J. Hamilton III); one of a single bird seen the following day (W.J. Hamilton III); one of a single bird *heard* September 19, 1976 (Janet McGee); and one of a bird found dead on October 11, 1976 (W. Bartush). Near Cache, in Comanche County, two were seen at night on October 3, 1977 (Jack D. Tyler). Edward D. Crabb collected a specimen in Canadian County in September, 1912. For Oklahoma County there are two records—one of a bird found dead near Lake Hefner on September 23, 1962 (John G. Newell), the other of a bird found crippled near Oklahoma City on October 4, 1978 (Elizabeth Black). For Cleveland County there are three records, all for the Norman area—one of a bird with a broken wing found October 7, 1974 (Patricia Bergey), one of a specimen collected October 13, 1959 (David H. Baepler), and one of a bird that must have injured itself flying into a wire or window on October 14, 1969 (Eugene Kendall).

No Common Poorwill thus far observed in the fall in Oklahoma has appeared to be in the least torpid. The latest date for the species is October 24. The poorwill found dead on that date presumably had been finding food along a road near Gate.

Common Poorwill, *Phalaenoptilus nuttallii*. New Mexico, 1981.
Dale A. and Marian A. Zimmerman.

Chuck-will's-widow

Caprimulgus carolinensis

In the early summer of 1952, while in Georgia making illustrations for Thomas D. Burleigh's book on the birds of the state, I became well acquainted with the Chuck-will's-widow. Several pairs of the birds nested on the Sherwood Plantation not far from the big house in which Herbert L. Stoddard, his wife, Ada, and I lived. We heard the "chuckers" every evening, several of them. Whether both males and females were calling, I do not know. At a nest (two eggs) that I found I made direct-from-life sketches of the incubating bird, the female.

Edward V. Komarek, whose Birdsong Plantation adjoins the Sherwood Plantation, tells me that the Georgia "crackers" transliterate the Chuck-will's-widow's cry as "Chips, dey fall outa de white oak," and that they often give the bird that name. Never do they call it the Whippoor-will (*C. vociferus*), for everyone seems to know that this much smaller species has a wholly different song. In Oklahoma, where the Chuck-will's-widow is fairly common in eastern and central counties and less common in heavy woods along streams westward to the Texas panhandle, it is usually called the Whip-poor-will, and I have had a hard time convincing people that the Whip-poor-will's song is a long-continued rapid repetition of a sprightly *whip-poo-weeah* that is quite different from the bigger species' clearly enunciated, rather deliberate *chook, weah, weah*.

In Georgia, I occasionally walked among the big pines just after nightfall with my flashlight, hoping to shine the eyes of the singing "chuckers." Following the birds about was easy, for the flashlight and I did not seem to disturb them. I never failed to marvel at the brilliant spot of orange-pink fire glowing off in the darkness as the big eye's *tapetum lucidum,* or shining carpet, reflected the flashlight's rays. I was to learn that much of the singing was done from the ground, but that certain birds had song-perches on dead or leafless branches ten to twenty feet up.

One bird that I often watched and listened to had such a perch. After calling several times this bird would flutter up and away, giving as it departed a series of weird sounds that I decided could not be vocal. They reminded me of the flicking of a whip or the breaking of a branch. I never was able to see the bird clearly while it was making the sounds, which I believe were produced by the striking together of the wingtips. The sound was so loud and sharp that I found it hard to believe that soft wing feathers could make it (see R.M. Mengel, R.S. Sharpe, and G.E. Wolfenden, 1972, *Auk*, 89: 440–44).

Another difficult-to-accept fact about the Chuck-will's-widow is that it eats small birds. Whether it catches these alive or finds them dead, it must swallow them whole, for it is not equipped with hooked beak and talons for tearing prey to pieces. If it does catch warbler-size birds alive, does the huge-mouthed "chucker" simply bolt such sizeable creatures while they are still struggling?

The question leads one to wonder about the Chuck-will's-widow's migrations. In Oklahoma, the species has been seen very infrequently in the fall. It is known to winter widely in Central America and South America. Does it, while moving southward, do so well above ground where, in the course of a night's travel, it may fly close to— even among—small birds that are also migrating? Capturing prey of this sort might be very easy for the Chuck-will's-widow. But we know so little about the bird's activities in the fall that all we can do is guess.

What I have just said makes clear that close observation is in order. In south-central Oklahoma several years ago, I happened upon an adult Chuck-will's-widow that was undergoing its late summer molt. The spot from which it flew was at the bottom of a steep-walled, well-shaded gully—

Chuck-will's-widow, *Caprimulgus carolinensis,* with egg and young.
Oklahoma, 1969. Frank J. Bunch.

the sort of place a human being would be unlikely ever to
visit, for it was hard to get down to. The bird had difficulty
flying, for many of its wing and tail feathers were missing
or only partly grown. I found nearly all of the molted tail
feathers at one end of a dry mud-bar at one side of the
gully's very bottom. Had these been molted over a long period, dropping out one or two at a time? Questions of this
sort are difficult, if not impossible, to answer. I could not
help believing that the bird had been spending the day at
that retreat week after week for some time.

Chimney Swift

Chaetura pelagica

So essentially aerial is this familiar bird that it must stay above ground if it is to survive. Its legs are so short and its jumping muscles so undeveloped that if forced to earth it has a difficult time flapping its wings hard enough to get

Chimney Swift, *Chaetura pelagica*. Ontario, Canada, 1982.
James M. Richards.

itself into the air again. Its four toes, though small, are very strong, and its claws sharp. The foot's clutching power is great—a fact known to all who have handled the bird; but it can't jump with its toes; they're not built for that. When a swift alights it is almost invariably near its nest on the inside of a chimney, hollow tree, well, or building. Clinging to a vertical wall it can use its wings in climbing upward or fall off with wings spread wide and fluttering, thus becoming airborne.

Throughout much of its range today, the Chimney Swift is a town bird, for the towns have most of the chimneys. In and near the village of Willis, in south-central Oklahoma, there are more old wells than chimneys, so the birds build their nests in the wells. Toward the end of summer, after the young swifts have learned to fly, certain wells are used as communal roosting spots. Here my students and I, using mist-nets, have captured dozens of the birds and banded them. Our procedure was simple. Waiting till after dark, we went to the well, held the stretched-out net over the entrance and ourselves, and dangled a nail at the end of a string into the well, thus stirring the birds up. When the nail reached the uppermost birds, they changed position, producing a muffled roar with their rapidly beating wings. As the nail moved lower, more birds were disturbed and there was another roar. Presently, the whole company was aflutter and moving upward toward the entrance. We could almost feel the wave of birds coming. Some of the swifts chirruped briefly. Out of the well they poured, flying into the net and alighting on our faces, hands, and clothing. Everyone had a chance to feel the strength of those toes and the sharpness of the claws and spine-tipped tails. To our delight we usually found a banded bird or two, individuals that had been captured near Willis in an earlier year.

Those powerful little toes have much to do with the Chimney Swift's reproductive success, for it is with them that the flying bird breaks off twigs for the nest. Nest-building proceeds soon after the species arrives from the south and it is carried on so unostentatiously that many observers who watch the birds swooping about, almost touching the trees, suppose that they are after insects. To see what is happening, one must watch closely. Through trial and error the birds have learned which trees have dead branches whose terminal twigs are brittle enough to snap off easily, so to trees with properly dead branches they go. They slow up just a bit as they reach the dead branch, grasp the twig with both feet, snap it off with a sudden twitch, and speed on. Now whether the flying bird passes the twig to its mouth, there to cover it with viscous saliva, I can't say. My eyes have not been good enough to see the transfer of twig to mouth; but by the time the swift gets back to its nest the twig probably has received the coating of saliva, for it must be added to the nest while the saliva still is moist.

The twigs that compose a swift's nest are invariably slender and not very long. Not any old twig will do. Cottonwood twigs are too thick. Sycamore twigs may not break off easily. Twigs that the swifts have been using on the campus during the past twenty years or so have been from Chinese elm and hackberry trees. And I have noticed, spring after spring, that certain trees seem to have dead branches on which the swifts depend. The salivary glands become enormous during the nesting season. Much saliva must be used when the first twigs are attached to the chimney. Wouldn't it be interesting to know how the nest of *Chaetura pelagica* evolved into the simple cupped bracket that we know so well today? Some of the world's swifts build nests of a wholly different sort. One Asiatic species makes its first nests of the season wholly of saliva. Bird's-nest soup, made of these nests, is said to be delicious. Did the far-back ancestors of the Chimney Swift evolve in such an unusual way as to find that they used *less* saliva if they made their nests of twigs? And how did they learn that they could break twigs off while flying rather than picking them up from the ground? Necessity has indeed been the mother of invention.

I continue to consider myself rather cowardly, for I have never boiled a few nice clean Chimney Swift nests and tasted the broth!

Chimney Swifts hatch naked. When partly feathered, they crowd the nest badly, especially if the brood numbers more than three. Equipped even at this early age with those strong toes and sharp claws, they climb out of the nest and arrange themselves under it. Their outcry when begging for—or receiving—food can be unbelievably loud.

Heavy rain can dislodge the nest and send the young ones to the bottom of the chimney. If they have not been chilled or weakened by starvation, they can be helped by holding them close to the bricks and allowing them to climb upward.

Ruby-throated Hummingbird

Archilochus colubris

There is something deeply appealing about the ruby-throat's smallness. How does the creature keep itself going? With feathers removed, it's not much larger than a bumble-bee, yet it has a heart that sends blood through an intricate skein of arteries, veins, and capillaries, lungs that put oxygen into the blood, and dermal papillae that, aided by what the blood brings them, produce feathers that make

Ruby-throated Hummingbird, *Archilochus colubris*. Ontario, Canada, 1982. James M. Richards.

101

flight possible, help to control body temperature, and flash color so spellbinding that the whole process of reproduction may depend on it. This last may sound like hyperbole, but watch a displaying male ruby-throat. See how that throat of his glows. And do not fail to see the entranced female as, moving her head back and forth like a spectator at a tennis match, she watches the male.

The ruby-throat is such an accumulation of wonders that deciding which ones are the most important is difficult. Those tiny wings, powered by muscles that attach to the sternum's deep keel, are said to beat eighty-five times a second in ordinary flight. This I have not checked myself. Stroboscopic photography has made the counting possible. No wonder those wings blur! Presumably they beat more rapidly if the tiny bird has to get somewhere in a hurry, less rapidly in moving upward or backward from a deep-throated flower, perhaps still less rapidly in rising from the ground.

From the ground? A hummingbird on the ground? All I can say in answer to this question is that on a hot summer day in southeastern Michigan, I stepped from waist-high weeds onto a country road to see a ruby-throat, with wings and tail spread, lying in the dust only a few feet from me. Thinking that it might have been hit by a car, I started to pick it up when suddenly those gossamer wings lifted and began to whirr, and off the bird went. I think it had been taking a sunbath or perhaps a dustbath.

Just how the ruby-throat migrates has yet to be ascertained. The species winters from Florida and southern Texas southward to Panama. Presumably it reaches the far parts of this winter range by easy stages, moving from flower-clump to flower-clump. In northeastern Mexico, I observed large numbers of ruby-throats, many of them molting young males whose grayish white throats were dotted with ruby spangles. Literally hundreds of these wintering ruby-throats fed around flowering trees along the Río Sabinas in southwestern Tamaulipas in the early spring of 1941.

Male ruby-throats return north ahead of the females. In Oklahoma, the vanguard appears in April and the birds may be seen feeding around the blooming redbud trees. When the females arrive the males display before them, and the females, following time-worn custom, proceed to select a nest-site and go ahead with building the nest and rearing the young without the male's knowing even where the nest is.

Those who watch ruby-throats at feeders are aware of the fact that there is no gallantry toward the females among the males. Each hummer, regardless of sex, is obviously there to satisfy its own appetite and there's nothing very reasonable about the incessant chasing. Presumably the birds are after what they need. We have a right to assume that all that activity is evidence of physical fitness, but is it not a great deal of energy wasted, badly wasted, as a result of this never-failing and tasty food supply? I'm not quite sure that feeders are "good" for hummers. They are an artificial element in the habitat.

Finding a ruby-throat's nest can be a memorable experience. One nest that I found was high in a big sycamore at the end of a dead branch that had caught on another branch when falling and had stayed there, swinging this way and that with every breeze. The swinging didn't bother the brooding mother or the young ones. It *did* bother every snake, squirrel, opossum or raccoon that happened by.

Female hummers seen regularly in towns are often not far from their nests, but the nests are hard to find. One summer in West Virginia, members of the Sutton household were all aware that a female hummer fed regularly among flowers in the yard. One day someone chanced to see her fly straight from the flowers to her nest on a horizontal elm branch only a few feet above the front walk. We and our friends had been walking under that branch for weeks without knowing that the nest was there. The two young in it were almost ready to fly.

Toward fall and departure for the south, ruby-throats store up fat for the long journey. Not necessarily do they attempt to travel in one jump from the northern limit of their breeding range (southern Canada) to Mexico or Central America, but the presence of the fat seems to indicate that migration makes special demands. Even the fattest ruby-throat that I have ever weighed—and I have handled many—weighed less than a nickel.

Red-bellied Woodpecker

Melanerpes carolinus

In Norman, central Oklahoma, where I have lived for the past thirty years, the red-belly has been one of my "home birds." No tree in my yard has been quite right for its nesting, but just across the street are four old maples of which it is fond. Seated on my front porch I can hear its *chiv-chiv,*

Red-bellied Woodpecker, *Melanerpes carolinus*. Arkansas, 1982.
E. Wayne Easley.

a note that often indicates excitement or annoyance, and its gentle *creer*, which connotes contentment, sounds a little like a song, and closely resembles one of the calls of the Red-headed Woodpecker (*M. erythrocephalus*). I have watched and listened to "my" red-bellies so often that I know about how things are going with them from their calls. If they cry *chiv-chiv* too loudly or too rapidly, I know something is wrong. If what drifts across the street to me is *creer*, I know that all is well. Both birds of the pair dig the nest-hole. When they relieve each other, the one that has been at work often flies to the top of the telephone pole on my side of the street and perches there long enough to give me a good look at the scarlet on its head and the black-and-white barring on its back. In the female only the back half of the head is red. I have not banded or color-marked these "home birds," but their behavior has been so much the same from year to year that I have come to think of them as my pair. They have shown a surprising preference for those four old maples. Not often have they visited the hackberry trees in my front yard, and never have I seen one of them in the big cedar of Lebanon in my backyard.

A non-migratory bird, the red-belly inhabits the southeastern United States, breeding northward to southeastern Minnesota and southern Ontario. It is not common along the north edge of its range. It digs its nest-hole in a dead stub, but often among leafy branches so that the entrance is not exposed. In this respect its nesting differs from that of the Red-headed Woodpecker, whose nests are often in telephone poles or wholly dead trees. Like the red-head it stores food—notably acorns.

Throughout the southern part of its range the red-belly regularly rears two broods. Young birds receive some insect food, of course, but when mulberries, cherries, wild plums, and chittamwood berries are ripe, these are often taken to the nest. A pair that I watched in south-central Oklahoma carried whole sand plums to a second brood of the season. How they disposed of the big seeds I do not know. When, after their twenty-four to twenty-six days as nestlings the brood fledges, they stay together, following their parents for about a month. When the whole family visits a mulberry tree, the young ones soon learn how to pull off berries without any help from their parents.

In Oklahoma the red-belly inhabits low-lying mature woodland virtually statewide, but is uncommon in the west where the big trees grow in strips along streams. It has bred at least once, and successfully, in the Black Mesa country at the northwest corner of the Panhandle (1960). In southwestern Oklahoma (Harmon, Jackson, Tillman, Greer, Beckham, Roger Mills counties) its range overlaps that of the Golden-fronted Woodpecker (*M. aurifrons*), a species that it resembles closely in some ways despite the striking difference in head-color. Where the two occur together they must be watched closely. They are said not to interbreed where their ranges overlap, but I suspect that where a shortage of one sex or the other develops in either species, mixed pairs result. In hybrid females some red should appear on the head. Another part of the bird to be watched is the rump, which is pure white in the golden-front, barred black-and-white in the red-belly.

On September 9, 1959, while J. David Ligon and I were watching and listening to the several red-bellies that were living among the big cottonwoods along the Canadian River in Ellis County south of Arnett, Oklahoma, we noticed that one bird of the area had a higher, sharper call than that of the others. What we had been hearing from the red-bellies was the familiar *chiv-chiv;* the different call sounded like *keef-keef* or *chef-chef*. The strange call was from a golden-front. I collected it, and also a red-belly, to establish the fact that the two species had been found together. The golden-front was in heavy molt.

107

Ladder-backed Woodpecker

Picoides scalaris

About seventy years ago, near Fort Worth, Texas, I saw my first Ladder-backed Woodpecker. It was busy whacking away at the bark of a thinly leafed tree that also was new to me, the mesquite. The bird was called the Texas Woodpecker in those days but, after seeing it several times in a mesquite, I fell to calling it the Mesquite Woodpecker. It was much like the Downy and Hairy woodpeckers (*Picoides pubescens* and *P. villosus*) but differed from them in having black-and-white bars on the back, and the red on the head of the male was a patch on the crown rather than a spot on the nape. The entrance to a nest that I found was about twenty feet up on the underside of a leaning dead stub.

Since boyhood, I have seen much of the ladderback in the Big Bend country of southwestern Texas, in Arizona, in many parts of Mexico, and in Oklahoma. "Mesquite Woodpecker" continues to seem a good name for it, not because it lives exclusively in the mesquite forest but because it seems to be the only woodpecker that regularly forages there. I have watched both flickers and Golden-fronted Woodpeckers alighting in a mesquite or looking for food on the ground under it, but they did not forage in the tree itself.

In Oklahoma the ladderback inhabits the Black Mesa country at the northwest corner of the Panhandle and the southwestern part of the main body of the state. In both areas, along with other woodpecker species, it forages and digs its nest-holes in many kinds of trees, especially cottonwoods and willows. In the Black Mesa country, it often forages also in the arborescent "cholla" cactus that is so conspicuous there. I have never seen a woodpecker other

Ladder-backed Woodpecker, *Picoides scalaris*. Oklahoma, 1984.
John S. Shackford.

than the ladderback foraging in a cactus of any kind in
Oklahoma.

I suspect that the ladderback has been a resident in the
Black Mesa country for a long time, for it is fairly common
there. It probably spread northward from low-lying, semi-
arid parts of Mexico along with plant life that found a suit-
able habitat north of the border. Its advent in southwestern
Oklahoma may well have been recent, for I know of no part
of that area in which it is really common. Scattered mesquite trees there are quite old, but there is no truly ancient
mesquite forest comparable to those of Mexico and southern Arizona. Much of western Oklahoma's grassland was

treeless, except along streams, until the mesquite arrived. When the mesquite came, the ladderback came too.

The spread northward of the mesquite deserves discussion, for the facts are extremely interesting. Much of the thin young mesquite forest that exists today in north-central Texas, in Oklahoma east of the Panhandle, and in southwestern Kansas owes its existence to cattle that were raised and driven north to Dodge City, Kansas a century or so ago. While mesquite seeds, swallowed whole, were passing through the cattle or horses, they received treatment that induced germination. On reaching the ground with the "cowflaps," under which the soil became damp, they quickly put down taproots long enough to reach water. Presto, more mesquite trees! Had there been no cattle, there might well have been few, if any, mesquite trees. Where there were mesquite trees, *Picoides scalaris* could thrive.

An ecologist may well ask, "Why, as the mesquite spread northward, did the Downy and Hairy woodpeckers not join with the ladderbacks in exploiting it?" The question needs an answer. Perhaps the ladderback drove competitors off. Perhaps the downy and hairy, content with what they had had for a long time, made no attempt to find out what a new tree was like. I have never seen a ladderback chasing any other kind of woodpecker as if trying to drive it off—and vice versa. More surprising, perhaps, is the fact that I have never seen a ladderback and a hairy or downy at the same time anywhere in Oklahoma. The statement carries weight, for I have spent much time afield in the state.

The only ladderback nest that I have found in Oklahoma was four feet up in a dead willow stub near a stream, but the stream ran through flat grassland that was studded with mesquite trees. A nest found by David F. Parmelee in southwestern Oklahoma was eighteen feet up in a slender cottonwood, again along a stream that flowed among scattered mesquite trees. A nest recently found by John S. Shackford and Warren D. Harden in Kingfisher County,

110

central Oklahoma, was in the main trunk of a mesquite about six feet from the ground. Most of the trees of that area were mesquites. To be noted is the significant fact that neither John nor Warren saw a Downy Woodpecker in those woods during the course of their several visits to the ladderback's nest. Warren believes that two woodpeckers that stopped briefly and flew on were hairies.

Both the ladderback and the mesquite forest are to be watched closely. One downy or hairy nest in a mesquite would invalidate some of what I have said.

Downy Woodpecker

Picoides pubescens

The downy is among the best known of North American woodpeckers, for it lives in towns as well as in wild areas, and it regularly visits window-feeders. In mature forests it seems to be less common than its larger cousin, the Hairy Woodpecker. According to my observations, it is not very common in southeastern Oklahoma's pinelands, and in western Oklahoma, in areas where the mesquite tree thrives, it is likely to be less common than the Ladder-backed Woodpecker. Notable is its custom of foraging among tall weeds, especially in fall and winter. In many parts of the United States I have watched downies flying from weed to weed, tapping the tough stalk here, finding something to dig for there, all as if among timber. Never have I seen a hairy finding food in this way; the hairy stays among the larger trees and does its foraging chiefly on the trunks and larger branches. Nor have I seen a downy climbing about in cactus, a favorite foraging-plant of the ladderback.

The downy is often seen in town. Everybody knows that males have a red spot on the nape that females lack. Downies are fond of suet and of sunflower seed. Sixty years ago, while my friend, Rudyerd Boulton, and I were both living in Pittsburgh, "Rud" invited me to spend a weekend with him and his parents at the family home in Beaver, thirty miles north of Pittsburgh. A high point of that pleasant visit was the hour we spent watching a male Downy Woodpecker that ate every sunflower seed a White-breasted Nuthatch (*Sitta carolinensis*) cached in the rough bark of a tree not far from the feeder. The downy moved out of sight to the far side of the tree while his provider

112

flew from the feeder with another seed, but the instant the provider started back for another seed, the downy went on with his thieving. It was all very amusing, for the nuthatch was dedicated to caching those seeds and the downy was equally dedicated to eating them.

An important reason for the downy's continuing abundance in Oklahoma is that its nesting and roosting holes are too small for the European Starling (*Sturnus vulgaris*). Larger woodpeckers, notably the Northern Flicker (*Colaptes auratus*) and the red-belly, are being eliminated by the starling. As for the Red-headed Woodpecker and the hairy, neither of which is very common in the state as a nesting species, I have no data clearly showing that starlings are to blame for their scarcity. Many redheads are killed because they are so slow in flying up from grasshoppers and other insects they find crippled or dead in the highway. And hairies seem never to be really common anywhere.

Downies are not very noticeable much of the time, but rivalry among males in spring makes them noisy as they display with wings and tail spread wide, calling *wickah, wickah* in a strident voice. When pairing is settled, the triumphant male gives a long series of *wickahs* as he flies off with his mate.

Nests of downies are usually in a dead stub, but one that I found near the university campus in Norman was in a living pine only four feet from the ground. At that nest I had a chance to observe the chicks, two males and two females, at close range. As fledging time approached, they became more and more noisy when sticking their heads out and calling for food. I continued to wonder why they were not caught by a cat. The crown-color of the males was pinkish red, of the females grayish white, a pattern believed by some to indicate that the downy's ancestors were more colorful than downies of today. A question that needs answering is this: Does the female downy drum, or is all the drumming done by the male? On a fine day in late winter—a day when the Carolina Chickadees (*Parus carolinensis*) are singing their full spring songs and a crocus or

Downy Woodpecker, *Picoides pubescens*. Arkansas, 1982.
E. Wayne Easley.

two may be up—I sometimes hear the drumming of three or four downies in my neighborhood. The drummers are never very close together and I never seem to be able to see them all. The ones that I see are males, but what about those that I fail to see or see only as they fly off? I continue to suspect that male downies do not do all of the drumming.

Both sexes work at the nest-hole and each sex makes its own roost-hole for the winter. These holes are important in the overall ecology of the area for both Carolina Chickadees and Tufted Titmice (*P. bicolor*) nest in them—not to forget the white-footed mice (*Peromyscus leucopus*).

114

Western Kingbird

Tyrannus verticalis

When the Western Kingbird returns to central Oklahoma in the second week of April, I know spring has come. The day may be chilly or windy, but there the pretty bird sits, atop the very tree in which it perched almost exactly a year before. It may look bedraggled, even dispirited, if wet, for Western Kingbirds like hot, really hot, dry weather, and they're not their truest selves when rained on.

Male birds usually show up ahead of the females and many of them may appear on the very same morning, as if a flock has flown northward together. If many males have arrived and the day is pleasant, the bickering begins. The several birds make clear to each other precisely where each plans to spend the summer. Breeding populations along

Western Kingbird, *Tyrannus verticalis*. Arizona, 1982. Betty Randall.

the Cimarron River at the west end of the Panhandle are so large that altercation among the newly arrived birds is downright noisy. They seem to be genuinely annoyed with each other.

When the females arrive and nesting starts, things settle down a bit. Nests are not hidden. They are not only in plain sight, but are so placed as to receive direct sunlight during part of the day. On the University of Oklahoma campus, a favorite nest-site is a partly dead Chinese elm branch well out from the trunk or a cross-bar on a utility pole. As the Chinese elms have died and been cut down, the kingbirds have switched to pines, hackberries, and sycamores. Nests in pines are usually well away from the trunk on a long branch or close to the tree's very top.

Nest-building is done by the female. She is well worth watching while she gathers material. The nest's foundation is of dried weed stems and slender twigs, its lining of dead grass, bits of wool, and roots. Why the roots are important I do not know, but spring after spring I have watched Western Kingbirds on the ground tugging at grass roots along the edges of bare spaces, especially those that landscape gardeners have dug around young trees. The kingbirds work hard at the roots, pulling and twisting and shaking the soil out. Twine is important, too, and dangerous. One day I found a dead female bird dangling at the end of a long piece of string. On another occasion someone called about a bird that was trying to free itself from a loop of cord around its neck. I got there just in time to save the kingbird's life.

Summer after summer a pair of Western Kingbirds have nested in a partly dead elm just across the street from the Stovall Museum. I have enjoyed watching the birds as they have carried food to their young. Both parents have learned that there is a dependable insect supply on the museum's south wall directly below a light that burns all night. The birds do not pick the insects up from the ground but find them on the wall or snatch them from the air.

116

The brood always takes its time in leaving the nest. Perhaps because of the heat and crowding, the oldest chick climbs to the rim, perching there for a day or so. Never, so far as I know, does it try its wings. Then another chick climbs out, even before its tail is more than a mere stub. Presently the nest is empty and the youngsters are lined up on the home branch close by, waiting for the return of a parent with food.

Finally comes the day when they leave the nest-tree, make their way across the street to a wire near the museum's south end, and sit there in a row about two feet apart, each with that fluffy, innocent look baby kingbirds have. Never have I witnessed that first flight. Does the whole brood take it at the same time? Do the parent birds nudge them into making it? Do they do any practicing at all, beating their wings or making short sallies out from the home-branch before they launch forth?

Now they are close to that good food supply. They watch passing butterflies and moths with real interest, as if half-resolved to go after them. They become used to human passersby, for the campus is alive with students that come and go. If someone tosses a pebble in their direction, they watch it almost wistfully as it moves higher and higher, stops ascending, and falls.

Soon the tails of the fledglings are full grown. They have learned by this time to catch some of their own food, but they still receive some from their parents. July passes. August arrives. And lo, the Western Kingbirds, almost to a bird, have left the campus. Why have they gone? Because there aren't enough insects? Probably they scatter widely waiting for the weather to become cool enough, or the days short enough, to start them on migration. They winter chiefly south of the United States, in middle America.

Scissor-tailed Flycatcher

Tyrannus forficatus

A puzzling fact about the scissortail is that it wears its finest plumage not in spring, while pairs are forming and nest territories are being established, but in the fall, just before it departs for its winter home in southern Mexico and Central America. In adults the molt into fresh plumage starts just after the young have left the nest. While it is progressing, great roosts, composed of old birds and young, form. The roosts assemble in the evening and disperse in the morning, scattering widely about sunup. The molt continues for some time. Until it has been completed, many birds in all age-groups are stubby-tailed and rather odd looking.

When molting is over, the longest-tailed birds are adult males. Birds with tails not quite so long are young males of broods that have just been reared. Still shorter-tailed birds are the adult females, and the shortest-tailed of all are the young females.

The early morning behavior of roosting birds is worth traveling a long way to see. Here in Norman, roosts have formed right in town year after year. As a rule, the roost is in a large tree. As the birds gather in the evening, they are not especially noisy, but in the morning there is considerable commotion as the adults, calling *pit, pit, pit-a-whit* in a spirited chorus, move restlessly from perch to perch, snapping their bills at each other. All at once the tree explodes as the birds, calling more loudly than ever, chase each other with tails opening and shutting as they move off in almost as many directions as there are birds, precisely as if each knew that obtaining food was an individual, not a communal, matter.

Scissor-tailed Flycatcher, *Tyrannus forficatus*. Oklahoma, 1976.
John S. Shackford.

I have followed some of these fall birds as they have left the roost. Presently each finds a fence wire, telephone wire, or dead tree from which to look for insects. As the sun warms things up, the insects begin to fly, and the hungry scissortails are busy. In this open habitat, there is likely to be some wind. The long tails of the perching birds are almost horizontal.

Departure for the south is not en masse, but presently the roosts break up and most of the scissortails that we see are perched on wires along the highways. They are comparatively silent at this time of year when away from the roosts.

The first birds to move north in the spring are the adult males, many of which are in such worn plumage that their tails are not very presentable. Now we hear the familiar *pit, pit, pit-a-whit* of a male on territory. His calling often starts so early that he is quite invisible in the darkness. He is on territory, to be sure, but does he have a mate?

The question is not an idle one. From what I have witnessed spring after spring in Oklahoma, I am inclined to believe that he is advertising for a mate as well as defending a territory that he had defended before. Female birds do not arrive with the males. Pairing must not take place, therefore, on the wintering ground. But I would not be greatly surprised to learn that breeding pairs are often composed of the very birds that have bred successfully at a certain favored spot, this regardless of how far apart the two may have been during the preceding winter. So powerful is the urge to return to the favored spot that males and females do so independently of each other; the early calling of the male convinces the returning female that she has come to the right place; the pair that bred there successfully meet once more; and the pair re-forms. Recovery of banded birds will be needed to prove all this, and getting proof will take time. If more adult birds can be banded, proof may come the more quickly.

The female builds the nest in an exposed position, often in a tree standing by itself in open pastureland. Most nests are well above ground, but one that I found in south-central Oklahoma was in a small mesquite only four feet up. The species is one-brooded as a rule, but two broods are sometimes reared. A female that I watched all season surprised me. Her nest was about five and a half feet up in a sapling persimmon. I watched her brood as they fledged. Not knowing that she was going ahead with a second brood, I paid the nest a perfunctory visit one evening, curious as to how the structure had stood the wear and tear of occupancy. Imagine my surprise when I found the female on the nest, with all of four chicks of the first brood ready to go to sleep within inches of her. The excited male parent scolded me from the top of a willow not far away. Four fresh eggs were in the nest.

120

The scissortail likes open country. It is not a woodland bird. Yet in Oklahoma's Panhandle, where the only woods are along the streams, the scissortail is not common. In the vicinity of Guymon, I have found one pair year after year. That pair has nested in a tree in an open field between the city and the well-wooded banks of the Beaver River. I have never found a nest in the vicinity of Boise City, and have not often even seen the species there.

Purple Martin

Progne subis

The Purple Martin, with its elegant ways, its fondness for birdhouses—some of which are embarrassingly ostentatious—and its cheery *putt-putt* and *ee-dip* cries, is one of North America's best-loved birds. Its popularity takes various forms. In Harrisburg, Pennsylvania, while I lived there as State Ornithologist from 1924 to 1929, a colony of the friendly birds occupied an unusually low birdhouse in front of a drugstore near the city's main square. The citizenry were so much interested in the colony that they kept close track of the birds' spring arrival from the south. In time, the tabulation of dates took a very human turn. People began betting that the martins would show up by a certain day. The return—or the failure of the martins to return—by that day made headlines in the newspapers. And speculators made, or lost, what might be called "martin money."

Those drugstore martins never brought out more than one brood in a summer. I didn't keep an eye on them myself, for I was usually off on expeditions at that season, but friends watched the birds for me. The species is widely believed to be one-brooded, but recent work with banded and color-marked birds in Texas has made clear that two broods are sometimes reared along the south edge of the breeding range.

Ascertaining the facts about two-broodedness is not easy. When first clutches of eggs are destroyed, second clutches often are laid, and if the date of this second egg-laying and hatching is very late, it's all too easy to assume that the nestlings are of a second brood, whereas actually they are of a delayed first brood. I have no data clearly in-

Purple Martin, *Progne subis*. Arkansas, 1984. E. Wayne Easley.

dicating that egg-laying ever takes place after normally early first broods have fledged. Those who study martins must bear in mind that subadult males look much like females. Pairs in which the male is subadult may start breeding late and young of such pairs may hatch and fledge so late that they appear to be of a second brood.

Only twice in my life have I seen martins using nest-sites not provided by their human friends. At Winnebago, Minnesota, where I lived for a short time as a boy, a small colony of martins nested somewhere in the narrow space between two frame buildings that abutted each other in the heart of town. I did not climb to the nests, but I saw the old birds flying in and out and watched the young after they had fledged. In Bethany, West Virginia, two pairs nested in old woodpecker holes in a tall dead stub along the edge of town. That was in 1914 or 1915, before the arrival of the European Starling in that part of the world.

If there are things about the martin's breeding season that puzzle me more than others, they have to do with the large dragonflies that the old birds bring to the nest toward the end of the fledging period. Eggs are incubated (by the female only) for fifteen to eighteen days; fledging requires almost a month more (J.C. Finlay, 1971, *Wilson Bull.*, 83: 255). In late summer, just before broods leave nests, really big dragonflies are brought to the young. The wings of the insects can easily be seen protruding from the beaks of the parent birds. Now where are these insects caught, in the

123

upper air? And is the whole insect swallowed by the young bird? If so, are the indigestible parts regurgitated as pellets? I have yet to see a parent martin battering a dragonfly roughly enough to break off those big wings, and I have yet to examine carefully a martin's used nest!

Another fact about the breeding season must be mentioned. The birds are fond of broken bits of clam shell. At Herbert L. Stoddard's Sherwood Plantation in southwestern Georgia, I never saw a martin on the ground unless it was picking up nest material or bits of clam shell. Neighbors had this comment: "It's the female birds that pick up the pieces of shell. They need it when they're laying eggs." Martins nested thereabouts in dried gourds hung in open spaces well away from trees.

At many a martin house the young birds have a distressing way of shuffling out of the compartment in which they have been living and falling to the ground—possibly as a result of the heat. The old birds circle about nestlings on the ground, chirping excitedly, but they do not take food to them unless the young ones find a weed or shrub to climb up on. Nestlings on the ground are, in other words, written off as done for.

At the end of the breeding season, young and old martins congregate in roosts before moving south. Some of the roosts are huge. One that has gathered year after year recently along the north shore of Lake Texoma, must have thousands of birds in it. Charles R. Brown, who has studied the martins intensively near his home in Sherman, Texas, has seen many martins moving northward across Lake Texoma to this roost at a season when one would expect them to be moving southward. A question that deserves an answer is this: Do very late broods migrate separately or does the roosting population's "mind" dictate that all broods be present or accounted for before the roosts break up and move southward?

Northern Rough-winged Swallow

Stelgidopteryx serripennis

The rough-winged swallow was just a name in a book for me until I was sixteen years old. The colored frontispiece in Chapman's *Bird-Life* showed four species of swallow, none of them the rough-wing. Chapman did mention the species, saying that it was a "more southern bird" than the Bank Swallow (*Riparia riparia*), "being rare north of Connecticut." Such statements didn't mean much in those days.

No, I was hardly aware of the rough-wing's existence until the summer of 1914, when, in West Virginia's northern panhandle, I found the species nesting in widely scattered pairs along Buffalo Creek, a beautiful, unspoiled tributary to the Ohio River. The first rough-wing that I shot for my collection was an adult male. The dead bird looked much like a Bank Swallow, but it had no dark band across its chest and its outermost primary had a fringe of tiny hooklets that felt like the teeth of a fine-tooth comb when I ran my fingernail along them. Even as I examined that first specimen, I wondered what the hooklets could be for. Were they for fighting, for digging the nest burrow? By this time I knew that rough-wings usually nested in burrows in vertical banks, though one pair that I knew about had its nest in a crevice in stonework at one end of a bridge and another pair had a nest in an old drain pipe.

If that first specimen had been a young bird in the plumage it would wear on its migration southward, I'd have felt no fine-tooth comb along its wing's edge. It would have been a bit more colorful, too, for the inner secondaries and greater coverts of the juvenal plumage are a warm brown, almost a rufous. Had the specimen been an adult female, there'd have been some roughness along the

Northern Rough-winged Swallow, *Stelgidopteryx serripennis*. Kansas, 1980. Orville O. Rice.

wing-edge, but not much, a circumstance suggesting that adult females may use those tiny hooklets more than adult males do or in ways that males do not.

As the years passed, I made some interesting observations, among them that when rough-wings returned to their nesting grounds, they were often in pairs. Not often did I see a single bird on that important arrival date in late April. Too, those early pairs were often flying about over the water not far from a burrow that rough-wings had used the previous summer. But were the two birds the very ones that had nested there? And if they were, had they dug the burrow or had they appropriated a burrow dug by some mammal or other creature whose habits I needed to know more about?

When I taught a course in bird study at the University of Oklahoma Biological Station along the north shore of Lake Texoma in south-central Oklahoma, I was fortunate in finding a breeding population of rough-wings close by. The several pairs were not a colony, for no two burrow entrances were at all close to each other. The burrows were in vertical earthen banks in heavily eroded pastureland well back from the lake shore. Each burrow was several feet up from the arroyo's floor and a foot or so down from pasture level. Had those burrows been dug by the swallows? My students and I decided that the birds must indeed have dug them, but we continued to wonder why we could find no accumulation of soil beneath the entrances. Could the swallows possibly have done the digging with their small, weak bills, carrying mouthfuls of earth off to be spat out well away from the nesting area?

I have been watching rough-wings for years. I have yet to see one of them picking at a spot as if starting a burrow, or flying from a burrow with a mouthful of earth, or kicking earth out while moving backward through a burrow. In short, I do not *know* how those burrows are dug. Bank Swallows have been observed starting burrows and kicking earth from burrow entrances while moving backward. Young Bank Swallows have been observed starting burrows not long after the broods have fledged.

So further observations are in order. And note that I have hardly touched upon the possible uses of that rough-edged wing. William A. Lunk, who made an exhaustive study of breeding Northern Rough-winged Swallows in southeastern Michigan some years ago, failed to find the birds putting the fringe of tiny hooklets to any obvious use. He finally decided—this part of his scholarly report delighted me—that the "most likely explanation" of the serrations was that they "form a mechanism for the production of some sort of sound." Then he proceeded to tell of four or five rough-wings, including two pairs, that were "swooping about with unusual vigor close to an available burrow where one pair was about to begin nesting" when he noticed "a rather shrill, quickly repeated whir or whistle." So those tiny hooklets along the wing's edge may be a musical instrument! Will the wonders of the evolutionary process never cease to take us by surprise?

Cliff Swallow

Hirundo pyrrhonota

According to my records the earliest spring date for the Cliff Swallow in Oklahoma is April 4. On April 4, 1958, Lawrence E. Dunn and I watched a huge colony of the birds building nests under a bridge across the Cimarron River, five miles west of Plainview, Woods County, northwestern Oklahoma. Every blessed bird seemed to be busy—another way of saying both males and females were gathering the mud. They continued to beat their wings while gathering it as if utmost haste were essential. Many of the nests were new, barely started, but the darkness of the wet mud on some made clear that many old nests were being repaired. The urgency to "get on with it" was, I believe, the result of built-in realization that unless they finished nest-building promptly, the mud supply would run out in this land of hot spells and long-continued drought. In Cimarron County, at the west end of the Panhandle, many a colony does not return to its favorite bridge, cliff, or culvert unless a mud supply is available when the birds return in the spring.

The birds that Larry Dunn and I saw on April 4 may have returned to their bridge before that date. Swallows migrate each day. Where those Plainview birds were on April 3, no one knows. But if they reached their bridge at a morning hour on April 4 and found the mud supply just right, they probably got to work. When, on that busy day, did they take time to go after food? Had pairs already formed? Larry and I should have stayed with them and learned some facts. One interesting thing I did learn: the birds did not continue to flutter merely to keep their feet dry; they often stood in the mud, gathering it in their

128

mouths while still fluttering. Never did one really alight. Too much time would be consumed by folding those long wings and spreading them again!

Cliff Swallows and Barn Swallows (*Hirundo rustica*) often nest together in big culverts, especially in southwestern Oklahoma. But the word *together* means one thing to the Cliff Swallows, something else to the Barn Swallows. Cliff Swallow nests abut each other, even overlap, often in long rows or clusters. Barn Swallow nests may be close to each other, but usually they do not touch. One feels that the Cliff Swallows depend on each other, would not even be there were it not for the presence of other Cliff Swallows, whereas the Barn Swallows, short of adequate nest sites, or opportunists of sorts, do not *need* other Barn Swallows close by, but develop a tolerance for them.

At one large, airy culvert near Madill, south-central Oklahoma, on July 8, 1959, I found nineteen Barn Swallow nests, each with eggs or young, and one Cliff Swallow nest, empty. Nor was a single Cliff Swallow flying about with the Barn Swallows. That one pair of Cliff Swallows evidently had built their nest and left when no other Cliff Swallows joined them. At an airy culvert near the village of Willis, in the same part of the state, a few pairs of Cliff Swallows nested in a solid row on one wall, while many Barn Swallow nests were scattered along both walls, all of them so close to the ceiling that the swallows had to squeeze in as they alighted. When we visited that culvert on June 21, 1968, we found a fairly large black rat snake (*Elaphe obsoleta*) curled up cozily in one of the Cliff Swallow nests. The snake had eaten one adult swallow and four eggs.

The Cliff Swallow is truly colonial; the Barn Swallow is not. Where many Cliff Swallows nest together, the reproductive cycle proceeds as if one organism, rather than many, were laying its eggs, hatching them, and fledging its young. Eggs and nestlings fall from the nests, the nests themselves fall, and there is some starting over, but not much. At one culvert colony in Cimarron County, nesting

Cliff Swallow, *Hirundo pyrrhonota*. Oklahoma, 1977.
John S. Shackford.

proceeded at so much the same pace that a total of seventy-nine young birds, all nearly fledged, were banded by Jack D. Tyler on July 3, 1971.

John Janovy, Jr., in his thought-provoking book, *Keith County Journal*, has a fascinating chapter on swallows. His sententious statement about the Cliff Swallow reads: "There is no such thing as a single Cliff Swallow." He might, of course, have said the same thing about the Barn Swallow or the Purple Martin (*Progne subis*), two other swallows that he discussed, but with those two species the relationship between individuals of nesting populations is much less close than the affinity that exists among Cliff Swallows. The Cliff Swallows, like their nests, crowd each other, in a sense overlap, in such a way as to make the colony a unit. Never have I seen a nesting population of Barn Swallows or Purple Martins, frightened by some sight or sound, suddenly form a cloud and move off en masse, out of sight, until the "colony mind" decides that return to the nests is safe.

Mixed populations of Cliff and Barn swallows deserve close study. From what I have observed during the past thirty years, I wonder if the Barn Swallow is becoming colonial in the southern Great Plains. Perhaps it is learning that nesting with, rather than separate from, other pairs has certain advantages.

Barn Swallow

Hirundo rustica

Whenever I think about this well-known, wide-ranging bird, which is called simply the Swallow in England, the image that crowds my memory is not of a twittering pair at their mud nest, but rather of a huge swarm of south-bound migrants feeding on insects forced from the weeds by flood waters along the north shore of Lake Texoma in south-central Oklahoma. The date: October 9, 1955. The knee-deep water was no longer rising. As I waded about I was surrounded by a veritable whirlwind of swallows, most of them Barns, plus a few Tree and Bank swallows (*Tachycineta bicolor* and *Riparia riparia*). Much of their prey they skimmed from the water. Moths, tree crickets, and craneflies that tried to alight on me brought the birds so close that I could hear the snapping of their bills. Knowing that swallows migrate by day, I wondered where all those thousands of birds would be roosting. Would it be on the sapling willows and persimmons among which I was wading, or on wires along a dirt road not far away? And how dark would it be when their quest for food stopped? I wish I had stayed there long enough to find out.

Another vivid memory is of a flock of about a hundred Barn Swallows, most of them young of the year, at rest on pavement that had once been a landing strip at Norman's airport. The date: August 29, 1961. The birds had been feeding around a pond close by, but now they were taking it easy. An area about fifteen feet square was fairly black with them. Not one was perched on a fence wire a hundred yards away. Had they chosen the ground to get out of the wind? Were they benefiting in some way from being close to the sun-warmed pavement? Had I put them to flight would they have left the place, heading southward en masse? I remembered that most premigratory flocks of Barn Swallows perch on wires, lined up close together, jostling for position, just far enough apart to allow quick spreading of wings for instant departure.

Of breeding pairs that I have observed, I remember most clearly one that I had been told had a nest in a big barn near Ligonier, Pennsylvania. I had no trouble finding the nest, for the swallows were doing their best to drive off a huge snake that was making its way to it above me by pressing its body against rafters about two feet apart. My sudden appearance, which had required opening a big door, startled the snake, which lost its grip, fell heavily to the floor, and slid off among bales of hay. The swallows continued their chatter a moment, then calmed down. A man below them on the barn's floor was nothing to become excited about.

In Oklahoma, Barn Swallows often nest close together, but the species can hardly be called colonial. Separate pairs nest on porches or in barns, but many pairs nest together in culverts, and culverts are so numerous that a large part of the Barn Swallow population breeds in them rather than in buildings. Nests in culverts do not touch each other, but they may be only inches apart and they may be close to Cliff Swallow nests if that species is nesting there too. Big Cliff Swallow colonies that nest under bridges or on canyon walls have no Barn Swallows with them, but in many culverts that I have visited, there have been both Barn and Cliff swallow nests, the latter invariably close together in a compact row.

These swallow aggregations, whether mixed or not, attract other animal life—snakes that prey upon eggs, nestlings, and adult birds; House Sparrows (*Passer domesticus*) that add feathers to the Cliff Swallow nests and dome-over the Barn Swallow nests with dead grass; mice that make themselves comfortable; and hordes of cimicid "swallowbugs" that swarm over the Cliff Swallow nests and crawl onto the investigator's hands as if eager to "get somewhere

Barn Swallow, *Hirundo rustica*. California, 1959.
Velma Harris, F.P.S.A.

else." I have not found these insects in Barn Swallow nests, but Cluff E. Hopla, the authority on avian ecto-parasites, tells me that under a bridge on the Wichita Mountains National Wildlife Refuge, he found swallow-bugs in several Barn Swallow nests—this despite the fact that the Cliff Swallow has not thus far been known to nest on that refuge. And Paul F. Nighswonger, who lives on his ranch near Alva, northwestern Oklahoma, has found swallowbugs galore in the droppings that have accu-mulated under Barn Swallow nests in his big barn. In 1975 he counted sixty-four nests there, at least thirty of them in use on May 21.

Is the Barn Swallow becoming colonial? In many parts of its range separate pairs have been the rule—one pair per barn, porch, mine-shaft, or bridge. Where two pairs have occupied the same barn, each pair has used its own win-dows or doors in coming and going. Is this sort of life-style changing? Is the Barn Swallow learning that nesting in groups, rather than in separate pairs, has its advantages? If the species does become truly colonial, will swallowbugs be part of its existence?

Blue Jay

Cyanocitta cristata

A feeling I have about Blue Jays is unlike any that I have about other birds. The Blue Jay is common. I see it every day in my yard, no matter what the season or weather. I know it well, so usually I am not surprised by its behavior or callnotes. But never do I see it flying just above the lawn with its gloriously blue, black, and white wings and tail full spread, or slipping off half visible through the shrubbery, or hopping with long, deliberate hops, carrying something in its bill; never do I see it *doing anything* without feeling that I must go on watching—without feeling that I must keep the bird in sight, lest I miss something important. Of course I feel this way about a bird I have never seen before or that I know is rare, but the jay is common, it's everybody's bird, it's almost a member of the household. Yet I know from experience that if I watch closely and continuously, I'll be witnessing the unexpected.

The other evening while eating supper in the kitchen, I saw a Blue Jay fly into the big cedar of Lebanon whose long branches almost touch the kitchen's windows. To my surprise the bird pulled a bagworm from the end of a twig, flew to a utility wire that passes through the branches, and proceeded to hold the well-protected larva in its left foot while it pounded, pounded, pounded, trying to get through to something edible. Knowing, as I did, how tough that bag was, I felt a bit sorry for the jay; but presently I saw it swallowing what must have been juice that had seeped through. I had never before seen a jay dispatching a bagworm. I suspect that the jay was a young bird that had much to learn. To be sure, a jay must eat. To be sure, a bagworm must outwit those who try to attack it.

136

Across the street from my house stand four old maples, in one of which there is a cavity about fifteen feet up that I can see clearly from my front porch in winter. Leafage hides the entrance in summer, but that fact does not annoy me, for it's only in winter that an Eastern Screech-Owl spends the day there. Usually the owl is gray, but now and then it's red, so there's no telling how many owls stop there as the season passes. The jays know about the owls and so do the squirrels. If I hear a squirrel barking near the cavity and see it flicking its tail, I know an owl's there. A jay hears the squirrel, comes by for a look, and presently there's a squirrel-jay rumpus worth listening to. While the noise continues I sometimes feel that the jays and squirrel are watching *me* to see what I'll do about the owl. Of course, this is just my imagination running wild.

Some years ago while with a class on a field trip to Canton Reservoir, I heard what I identified as the trilling of an Eastern Screech-Owl in a tree not far from the lake shore. The sound surprised me, for the day was bright, but I told the class to surround the tree, look hard, and find the owl. We all looked and looked . . . and looked. No owl. Whereupon out flew a Blue Jay that repeated its most derisive shrieks, precisely as if laughing its head off at us. We should have followed that jay awhile just to see what trick it might pull next.

I'm used to telephone calls about jays, most of them about baby jays that have left the nest while still unable to fly. Jays, being jays, are adventuresome no matter how young, so to the ground the babies go, where they're lucky if a cat doesn't find them. One call that came from a man recently started off with a question: "Do you know how bad these jays are?" I replied that I had known jays a long while. Whereupon he went on: "Do you know what that jay did? It went to the martin house and stuck its head in and pulled out one of the baby martins and flew off with it right in front of all of us. I had no idea jays were that bad!" All I could say was that even as we human beings like young chicken fried, so do jays like young martins raw.

137

Blue Jay, *Cyanocitta cristata*, at its nest. Ontario, Canada, 1983.
James M. Richards.

A favorite spot for the jays in my yard is under the big cedar of Lebanon. The accumulation of needles there makes the soil very loose and the jays like to bury acorns and pecans in it. Neither oaks nor pecan trees grow in my yard, so the jays bring their treasure from afar. They bury it carefully two or three inches down. Every summer I pull up little saplings, for the jays never dig up what they've buried. They are planting trees that will produce food for future generations. But when jays fly off with their gullets packed full of sunflower seeds, are they going to plant them somewhere?

American Crow

Corvus brachyrhynchos

The crow is intelligent. Those who have studied it in field and laboratory tell us that it can count up to three or four; that it has a vocabulary of twenty-some sounds; that it can solve simple puzzles and work its way out of predicaments. Most of us know that it is too smart to be struck by traffic. Keen of eyesight and hearing, it leaves the carcass on which it is feeding long before it really needs to. Never, while driving, have I come close to hitting a crow. Indeed, only once have I handled a crow that had been killed by traffic. That bird was young, not young enough to have

American Crow, *Corvus brachyrhynchos*. Oklahoma, 1976.
John S. Shackford.

139

grayish-blue eyes, but obviously not long out of the nest. The man who brought it to me almost apologized for the crow: "It's the only crow I ever hit. There were three or four young ones eating the dead rabbit. This one just wasn't fast enough!"

The crow is intelligent enough to sense the advantages of joining forces in a common cause. Pairs are territorial, so nest well apart as a rule, but they do not hesitate to form mobs if a big owl is to be driven off. We who listen can tell when a crow has found an owl and we are not surprised as we hear the other crows gathering. A sudden burst of short caws—that must mean something like "Give it to him, boys!"—and we know that the owl has been routed.

Crows join forces when finding food, too. Several summers ago while I was finishing a manuscript in Norman, I went to the campus early each day for a cup of coffee at the Student Union. I arrived at the Union about the time five crows did, all of us on schedule. The crows, possibly a family group, had learned that there was food along the sidewalk near the cafeteria's entrance if only they could get to it before the janitors did. Their approach was cautious, but they found that I was harmless so proceeded with their search for edibles almost as if I weren't there. They found a good deal—popcorn, potato chips, parts of ice cream cones. The contempt with which they flicked aside a paper cup that had nothing in it was amusing. Call this humanizing if you like; what I saw certainly reminded me of human beings.

The way in which crows tolerate each other in winter is impressive. Watch them feeding in a stubble field. There seems to be no sparring, no undignified rushing after the scattered kernels, no hint of the greediness that is so characteristic of European Starlings whatever the season. For crows, winter seems to be a time for enjoying each other, for conviviality.

Toward nightfall in winter the roosts gather. Well filled with food that they have found, the scattered flocks move toward the woods in which roosts have gathered year after

140

year. The food they have eaten is important. Knowing just how to obtain that food is important. If food happens to be thirty, forty, or fifty miles from the roost, so be it. The birds travel great distances if they have to, but there has to be a reckoning, metabolically speaking: the longer the flight to and from the roost, the more food they must eat. I believe I have never collected in winter a crow specimen that was fat.

The crow is hardy. It is found all year in many parts of North America, but it is not built for bitterly cold winters. Its tarsi and toes are completely unfeathered. In most of Canada it is migratory. The northern limits of its winter range stretch across the continent from Vancouver Island to New York. From these limits southward there are roosts, some of them huge beyond belief. One such roost is at Fort Cobb Reservoir in southwestern Oklahoma. Here the gunners gather year after year and the killing goes on—partly in the name of conservation—for the crow is known to eat quail and pheasant eggs, not to forget young cottontails and other small mammals valued as game.

The crows at the Fort Cobb roost have been studied. Robert Kinneburgh, who has been visiting the roost for years, has made one intensely interesting observation. In the severe winter of 1978–79 when the whole reservoir froze over, the crows—gathered close together on the ice—so warmed the ice that it melted, furnishing them with much needed drinking water.

White-necked Raven

Corvus cryptoleucus

In all Oklahoma counties bordering the Texas Panhandle, the White-necked Raven is a fairly common bird in summer. In southwestern Oklahoma it breeds eastward along the Red River as far as Jefferson County, but its eastern limits in the area north and west of that county are ill-fated. In far western Oklahoma it is common in the flat land around Boise City, but twenty miles or so west and north of Boise City, where the rough Black Mesa country begins, a big cousin, the Common Raven (*C. corax*), takes over. Throughout the white-neck's Oklahoma range another congener, the American Crow, also breeds, but that species keeps to the woods along the larger streams, avoiding the cultivated fields and open grassland. The white-neck is a little larger than the American Crow; it has a heavy, rather blunt-looking bill; the feathers of its neck and breast are pure white basally; its cry is a dry *kronk*, not a *caw;* and it soars more often than the American Crow does.

The extensive area mentioned above is the white-neck's summer home, but nowhere in Oklahoma is the species known to be present the whole year. The facts are puzzling. The white-neck certainly appears to be as tough a bird as the American Crow, yet that species fairly swarms in winter in parts of Oklahoma—for example, the Fort Cobb reservoir area in Caddo County—that have no white-necks at all at that season. Do considerable numbers of white-necks pass through the state on their way to and from wintering spots? If so, why have these flights not

The most recent edition of the *Check-list of North American Birds* (1983, American Ornithologists' Union) uses the English name Chihuahuan Raven for this species.

White-necked Raven, *Corvus cryptoleucus*. New Mexico, 1983.
Dale A. and Marian A. Zimmerman.

been reported? Was the flock of about two hundred white-necks that John S. Shackford and I observed on August 29, 1963, a few miles east of Boise City, preparing to move southward en masse to the vicinity of Vernon, Texas, where white-necks are said to winter in great numbers, or north-westward to Liberal, Kansas, where Lawrence Herbert watched thousands of the birds passing back and forth over his house throughout the fall and winter of 1979–80? These wintering populations must establish themselves where there is an ample food supply. Precisely what they eat at these favored spots, not one of which is known to be in Oklahoma, remains to be ascertained.

All who are familiar with the "shinnery country" of

Ellis and Roger Mills counties and with the comparatively treeless parts of the Panhandle, know how easy it is to find White-necked Raven nests. There are only a few trees along the Panhandle's highways and these aren't very large as a rule, yet in them are white-neck nests. Climbing to the nests is easy. Where there aren't any trees, the nests are on windmills or telephone poles, and such nests are often made largely of old barbed wire. At one of these wire nests, placed on a transformer near the top of a utility pole, my friend David F. Parmelee received an unpleasant shock—one strong enough to make the two of us wonder how the white-necks carried on without being electrocuted.

Now for a bit of white-neck behavior that deserves careful attention. Almost fifty years ago, when I saw much of the species in the vicinity of Marathon, Texas, I became convinced that during courtship males (and perhaps females also) would, while facing the wind, turn their heads in such a way as to permit the neck feathers to blow up, revealing the snowy white. I saw the white so often that I decided the birds were using the wind in showing off. In Oklahoma I haven't often observed what appeared to be courtship behavior, but more than once, while traveling on the highways of Texas and Cimarron counties, I have seen sudden flashes of white from white-necks feeding in the fields and I couldn't help feeling that the flashes were more than accidental. They reminded me of signals from a heliograph.

Carolina Chickadee

Parus carolinensis

This easily identified bird is the darling of every man, woman, or child who runs a window-feeder. There is something winsome and wholehearted about the little creature with black cap, black bib, and white cheeks that flies in so boldly, carries off another sunflower seed, and pounds away until the tough husk falls off.

So common is the Carolina Chickadee in the main body of Oklahoma (westward to the Panhandle), even in towns and residential parts of the largest cities, that we may all too easily assume that the species needs no further study. We see it every day, especially in winter. We often hear the *chick-a-dee-dee-dee* call for which it is named. And, on one of those sparkling January days when there is not a flower in sight, we hear the tuneful, four-noted song that predicts the return of spring. On that very day the Downy Woodpeckers are likely to be beating their dead-stub drums.

The spring song announces establishment of territory, the formation of a pair or continuation of a pair-bond, and possibly even the finding of a cavity in which a nest will be built. Often the cavity is an old woodpecker hole. If the chickadees can't find a cavity to their liking, they dig one themselves, and they both work hard, making the tiny chips fly. Nests that I have found have been from three to about forty feet up. They are usually in a tree but sometimes in a fencepost. Nest-building may start long before the weather feels warm enough for that sort of thing. I suspect, too, that the nest may be built well before egg-laying starts, but this part of the reproductive cycle needs further study. A "rest period" between nest completion and egg-laying is of frequent occurrence in the bird world.

A nest found April 3, 1916, in northeastern Oklahoma held seven eggs, probably a complete clutch. One found on April 3, 1953, in southeastern Oklahoma held four eggs, probably an incomplete clutch. Once egg-laying starts, an egg is laid every twenty-four hours, and incubation probably does not start until the clutch is nearly complete. A nest found April 22, 1960, in central Oklahoma held six heavily incubated eggs. One found April 29, 1935, near Tulsa held six eggs—an unusually late date for eggs. Recently fledged broods have been seen in central Oklahoma on April 26 in 1980 and 1981, in southeastern Oklahoma on May 26, 1954, and in northeastern Oklahoma on May 28, 1953. Late broods may well be "delayed"—that is, hatched from eggs laid after the early first clutches have come to grief.

There is no shred of evidence that the Carolina Chickadee raises two broods a season in Oklahoma. This is puzzling, partly because the species is common and partly because there should be no food problems for second broods. As we study the matter, we cannot help wondering whether two-broodedness would bring to Oklahoma's woodland habitat too many chickadees. The thought is preposterous. How could there be too many of those fine little birds? Perhaps we should be content with things as they are. Downy Woodpeckers now provide many holes in which chickadees can nest. There probably are enough woodpecker holes for both chickadees and Tufted Titmice. If there were too many chickadees, perhaps the Tufted Titmice would be crowded out—or vice versa. Balance may well be essential. The tufted tit, too, is one-brooded.

Getting information on a nestling chickadee's life is not easy, for no one wants to tear open the nest hole. The fledging of a brood has been witnessed many times. But who knows what goes on in the crowded nest-hole as the several chicks become larger? Do they exercise their wings preparatory to taking that first flight? Do they grab at each other to strengthen their toes?

146

Carolina Chickadee, *Parus carolinensis*, young, Arkansas, 1976.
E. Wayne Easley.

On April 26 in both 1980 and 1981, William R. Johnson witnessed the fledging of a brood at the same nest-hole in his yard in Norman. In 1981 he captured the last of the brood as it flew in a straight line from the nest. It flew as if it had been flying all its life. Yet not one of its flight feathers was fully grown. Every primary wing feather, every secondary wing feather, and every tail feather was sheathed for a considerable distance at the base.

No wonder those fresh-from-the-nest young birds look stub-tailed: they *are* stub-tailed! Are they truly fledged? Well, at least they can fly, and they can clutch a perch with their strong toes, and they soon learn what it takes to be a chickadee by trouping through the woods with their par-

147

ents. The family groups go about together all summer long.

A closely related species, the Black-capped Chickadee (*P. atricapillus*) may occasionally move into Oklahoma from the north in winter. That species has a two-noted *phee-bee* spring song and its secondary wing feathers have noticeably whitish edgings. It is both actually and proportionately longer-tailed than the Carolina Chickadee.

Rock Wren

Salpinctes obsoletus

"That bird's building a nest," I shouted. "Find a comfortable spot and sit down right away. We must find the nest." My audience, strewn about me on the rocky slope, were members of the Oklahoma Ornithological Society who were climbing to the top of the Black Mesa with me. The spot was a mile or so east of the New Mexico state line; the date May 13, 1961; the bird a Rock Wren with a tuft of dead grass in its bill.

The wren was a bit flustered, but it did not drop the grass. Presently it flew to a big rock about twenty feet downslope, hopped from rock to ground, looked the closest of us over carefully, and disappeared under the rock. "That's where its nest is," I shouted. "But stay where you are. We want to see what happens." What I was hoping for was a glimpse of a Rock Wren lugging in one of those flat stones that it places near its nest as a sort of pavement. Many such stones appear to be too heavy for a Rock Wren to carry. Might two Rock Wrens, working together, carry in extra big stones? I wondered, too, about the pavement. Why should it be there? Of what use was it?

The wren brought no more material for the nest, whose well-lined cup we could feel back under the rock. Nor did it bring in a paving stone. Upslope a way a male wren started singing. A phrase repeated several times sounded like *ti-keer*. Neither wren of the pair scolded us.

We found two more Rock Wren nests that day, not on top of the mesa, but near the foot. One, with several small young, was under the lower end of a huge rock. Leading up to it was a pavement of about twenty small flat stones that evidently had been put in place with care. The other

149

nest, possibly deserted, held one egg, a cowbird's, and there was no pavement.

Nesting may, for some reason, be later in spring in the Black Mesa country than in other parts of Oklahoma. On May 13, 1962, James L. Norman watched five recently fledged Rock Wrens and their parents flouncing up and down a rough slope near the Tenkiller Reservoir dam in Sequoyah County, far eastern Oklahoma. The sighting did not greatly surprise him, for he had seen an adult Rock Wren carrying a fecal sac on the same slope fully three weeks earlier (April 22). Egg-laying at that nest must have started very early in April, perhaps in late March.

The Rock Wren is a western bird. Oklahoma's Black Mesa country, the arroyos and "breaks" in more eastern parts of the Panhandle, and such rough terrain as the Antelope Hills, Glass Mountains, and Wichita Mountains in the western half of the main body of the state, all seem right as habitats; but when the bird shows up in the forested eastern third of the state it seems out of place. How does it happen to be there? Has its real habitat, the semi-arid west, become overcrowded?

Some facts about Rock Wren distribution are in order. In some parts of the species' extensive range it breeds from below sea level (Death Valley) upwards to tree line and higher in the mountains, a truly spectacular altitudinal summertime range. Any bird with that sort of breeding range must have a capacity for adjustment to the vagaries of temperature, wind, rainfall, etc. That very capacity may make of it an "explorer" species (i.e., one prone to wandering about in search of areas in which it can nest). Sightings in central and eastern Oklahoma make clear that Rock Wrens show up almost anywhere, providing the spot is "rocky" enough.

Every big impoundment in Oklahoma has a dam that is "rocky," and therefore western, in certain ways. No wonder the explorer Rock Wrens find themselves comfortable near them. Even the glare of the concrete on hot summer

Rock Wren, *Salpinctes obsoletus*. Oklahoma, 1981.
Joseph A. Grzybowski.

days probably seems just right to them. So pairs form, nests are built, young are reared, and lo, we have a western species breeding extralimitally.

I well remember what I have called my "Rock Wren day" (September 30, 1965) on the university campus in Norman. I was at work in my Bird Range, a one-floored building flanked on the north by a graveled parking area. A student knocked, opened the door, and said, "There's a strange bird out here." I found the bird without trouble. It was scuttling about on the concrete parking blocks that kept cars from driving onto the grass. We saw it catch and eat a grasshopper. It was a Rock Wren and it was miles,

151

literally miles, from anything that might be considered proper Rock Wren habitat, but the gravel and concrete blocks were "rocky" and the wren seemed to be at home with them.

The photograph taken by Joseph A. Grzybowski shows a Rock Wren with a big dragonfly. The young wren that tried to swallow that insect whole must have had a hard time. I cannot help wondering how the wren happened to catch it. The photograph was taken in the Black Mesa country where I haven't seen many such big dragonflies.

Canyon Wren

Catherpes mexicanus

The poet William Wordsworth, recalling how often he had heard England's famous cuckoo and how infrequently he had seen it, asked whether he should call the creature a bird or "but a wandering voice." There are times when I feel precisely that way about the Canyon Wren. I hear the little bird's song over and over. The seven or eight descending notes shatter the silence of the wild place. I look and look for the singer but can't see it high or low. The song is there, but the singer isn't.

The song is remarkable in several ways. Saying that it comes "tripping down the scale" may not be wholly accurate from the physicist's or musician's standpoint, but the wording sounds right. The song's ending, an ascending trill quite different in character from the loud notes preceding it, sounds almost apologetic, as if the bird were saying, "Don't pay too much attention to the blast you've just heard. I have my lighter side, you know!"

If, as one author has stated, "the female sings quite as much as the male" (W.E.D. Scott, 1885, *Auk*, 2:351), we must revise our concept of the male as sole defender of territory with the comment that since Canyon Wrens are hard to see, perhaps the singing of both sexes helps the pair to keep track of each other. To be borne in mind while investigating this matter is the possibility that two songs heard not far from each other might be those of rival males rather than of a pair. I have never collected a singing bird that proved to be a female.

Like the Rock Wren, the Canyon Wren is western. It ranges from southwestern Canada southward to Central America, its habitat requirements north of Mexico being rather strict, but less so in Mexico and Central America. I well remember the odd feeling I had at the Estación Limnológica in the city of Pátzcuaro, southwestern Mexico, when, inside one of the two-story buildings where the doors and windows were open most of the time, I watched a Canyon Wren singing. Even in that not very spacious building the song's clear notes reverberated. The nest was in a hole in an inside wall, so the birds came and went, often carrying big spiders to the nest and white fecal sacs away from it. The fecal sacs were taken quite a way from the building before being dropped.

According to my observations during the past thirty years, the Canyon Wren is strictly nonmigratory in Oklahoma. In this respect it differs from the Rock Wren, which probably moves southward to some extent in winter. Unlike the Rock Wren, the Canyon Wren is not an "explorer" species. It does not pop up unexpectedly in places that resemble canyons to some extent. Not a single Oklahoma record for *Catherpes mexicanus* is in any way comparable to that of the Rock Wren that appeared on the university campus in Norman.

I was surprised to find the Canyon Wren common in the Wichita Mountains, for no canyon there is very deep. The Wichitas will be furnishing some ecologist of the future a wonderful spot for the study of wrens, for in the vicinity of Mount Scott the Canyon, Rock, Bewick's (*Thryomanes bewickii*), and Carolina wrens all breed unless a hard winter has killed the Carolinas off, and I suspect that even the House Wren (*Troglodytes aedon*) breeds there from time to time, despite the hot dry weather of some summers.

No one has made a close study of Canyon Wrens in Oklahoma, but I believe the species is regularly two-brooded here. On April 26, 1959, William E. Southern found a nest "in a crevice between rocks" just below the top of the Black Mesa. Two "barely fledged young" seen on May 16, 1957, by Julian A. Howard in the Wichita Mountains Wildlife Refuge headquarters building were undoubtedly a first brood for the season. A nest (three

Canyon Wren, *Catherpes mexicanus*. Oklahoma, 1981.
Joseph A. Grzybowski.

eggs) found by R. Crompton Tate on June 11, 1920, in Cimarron County, two young "just out of nest" seen in Kiowa County by J. David Ligon on July 10, 1960, and four young "just out of the nest" observed by Dan F. Penney in the Wichita Mountains on July 14, 1965, were probably all of second broods.

A Canyon Wren undergoing its complete molt in late summer and early fall may, I believe, become flightless for a time. A bird that I observed in a canyon four miles south of Kenton on September 3, 1971, refused to fly even when I approached it closely and tossed a pebble at it. Instead, it climbed from rock to rock until it was almost out of sight well above me. I suspect that it was unable to fly.

Bird students often think of late summer and early fall as a "slack" period and therefore do not pay much attention to birds during these seasons. Canyon Wrens are hard to see at best, and molting ones can slip in and out among rocks without leading one to wonder whether they are flightless or not.

155

Carolina Wren

Thryothorus ludovicianus

This nonmigratory bird of the southeastern United States I have seen much of in Florida, Georgia, West Virginia, Texas, and Oklahoma. It is a popular species, for it inhabits residential parts of towns as well as wooded lowlands, and it sings brilliantly. It does not often nest in birdhouses. If roomy houses designed for it were placed in hidden away places under porches or in sheds it might use them, but people like to see the houses they provide for birds.

The male Carolina Wren sings all year and in all kinds of weather, though infrequently in late summer while the molt is on. His song has won for his species such nicknames as "teakettle bird." I know, from listening carefully, that the three-times-repeated phrase of an average song varies considerably: sometimes it sounds like *which jailor, which jailor, which jailor* or *pea-deedle, pea-deedle, pea-deedle*. The singer performs with his head up and tail hanging straight down. When not singing he goes about much of the time with his tail up—as most wrens do.

The female is said to sing, but she evidently does not do so regularly. She does have an almost comical *djeer* that is not a scold, that she often gives in a kind of duet with her mate, and that sounds as if she's poking fun at him for declaring himself so boisterously. Both birds have a rough scolding note that is instantly recognizable as such.

In southern parts of the species' range, nesting starts early and two broods are reared. Nests are bulky, sometimes filling one corner of a box left lying under a porch or the deep-freeze part of a refrigerator discarded with door open. The somewhat domed-over nest-cup is lined with

156

fine dry grasses, roots, and leaf skeletons, but not with feathers. Nests away from town are usually in shady parts of bottomland woods near a stream, placed in a low crotch on a vine-covered branch in a fallen dead tree, or among the leaf-litter on a sloping bank.

Many nests are parasitized by Brown-headed Cowbirds. One such nest in central Oklahoma was in a doll's house about three feet from the window through which the wrens were obliged to go in reaching it. The cowbird must have used all the courage she possessed in finding it, for cowbirds usually avoid complicated nest-sites. This particular cowbird did not, apparently, remove a wren's egg before depositing one of her own. At any rate, no one found the remains of a wren's egg on the floor of the doll's house.

In the city of Norman, Oklahoma, the Carolina Wren was fairly common from the fall of 1952 to the fall of 1978. Nests that I knew about were in vines covering the side of an old building, in potted ferns on porches, and on shelves in garages. One, in a woodpile in a neighbor's yard, I did not try to find lest I cause the birds to leave, but the singing of the male told me that he was "on territory." We all knew from the loud scolding about where the nest was, and everyone rejoiced when the five young wrens appeared, no cowbird among them!

All went well in Norman until the winter of 1978–79, a season that must have been too much for the Carolina Wrens, for not since then have I heard a male singing in my neighborhood, nor has anyone reported seeing the species anywhere in the city. I suspect that the snow with its hard crust, the low temperatures, and the gusty winds killed the wrens outright. I wish we had watched them as they sought shelter. Some of them must surely have visited feeding counters, and these we might have followed about until dark. Everyone must have assumed that since the wrens had always been here in winter they were built to withstand the weather, no matter how bad it might be.

Carolina Wren, *Thryothorus ludovicianus*. Georgia, 1983.
M. Alan Jenkins.

Had we followed them to their roosting spots we might
have found them alive or dead in clusters—evidence that
they had joined forces to conserve their body heat.

George A. Hall tells me (letter of October 1, 1981) that
in northern West Virginia "the winter of 1977–78 was a
bad one and the Carolina Wren population was greatly reduced. The following winter . . . was even worse and . . .
just about finished them off at most places. They are making a slow comeback."

My guess is that the Carolina Wren is not very well
feathered. Some birds, notably the American Goldfinch
(*Carduelis tristis*), have a great many more feathers in winter than in summer. But no one seems to have counted a
Carolina Wren's feathers at any season. For a comparative
feather-count, two specimens will have to be collected, one
in summer, one in winter. Feather-counting is not easy: if
it's not done with great care, there's no point in doing it.

American Robin

Turdus migratorius

When my father discussed birds with me in those early Nebraska days, he was never flippant. One late afternoon in early summer when he was about to mow the lawn and I was digging up dandelions, he asked me if I'd ever noticed how a robin cocks its head to one side as if listening for the slightest sound. "Son, what's it doing? Can it hear those worms down under the grass?" I may not have replied, for assuredly I did not know whether a robin could hear an angleworm shoving its way through the soil; but the question put me on the spot as a scientist, and I found myself watching robins as I'd never watched them before.

They *did* look as if they were listening. And often, after standing quite still in one spot for a while, they would

American Robin, *Turdus migratorius*. Oklahoma, 1984.
John S. Shackford.

159

pounce suddenly forward, grab a worm at its front end, pull all five or six inches of it out, whack it a bit and gobble it down, or make a wriggling mouthful of it and fly to the nest where the hungry young ones were waiting.

Frank Heppner, experimenting with thirteen robins in California, found that they did not hear the worms, but saw them. His studies included analysis of the earthworms' burrowing sounds with an audiospectrograph. "The intensity of the noise inherent in the recording instruments was below the minimum sensitivity level of the audiospectrograph (F. Heppner, 1965, *Condor*, 67: 247–256). Let no reader assume from what has just been said that robins have poor ears. They hear extremely well. A loud kissing of the back of the hand, in imitation of a young bird in distress, will bring an irate robin close in no time, and if the imitation is convincing enough, more robins gather, and presently all the birds of the neighborhood, even the jays, are voicing their protest. It's a good way to find out how many birds, and of what species, live close by.

The robin is wonderfully adaptable. I have found it nesting at sea level in Delaware; at the northern limit of trees on the Labrador coast and at Churchill, Manitoba; in Mexico's mountains at elevations from seven to twelve thousand feet; and in semiarid country at the west end of the Oklahoma Panhandle.

At Norman, in central Oklahoma, it is by far the commonest bird of the university campus in summer. The thirty or so pairs that nest there raise two broods each year; the territories fit closely together; the males are aggressive in defending these, so all summer long we see males chasing each other about, occasionally witness a real fight, and hear snatches of song.

One or two pairs—of older birds probably—begin nesting in advance of the others, and these will have their young out so early that we can't help wondering whether they will rear three broods rather than the usual two. Most of the population starts nest-building when warm weather is assured, and thought-provoking it is to see female after female at work on her nest precisely as if the warmth of the sun or dew on the grass or some other element of the environment had affected one and all in precisely the same way. Presently every nest that we know about is finished. There may or may not be a "rest period" before egg laying begins, and then there are eggs (for the Blue Jays to steal) all over the campus. The season is on, really on.

Robins nest in many parts of Norman, but the concentration I have mentioned is on the campus. One or two pairs nest in or near my place, so robins after worms or feeding their stub-tailed fledglings in my backyard are a familiar sight. The old birds feed the young for several days after the brood leaves the nest, but force them to be "on their own" about the time their tails reach full length. It is amusing to see a parent, worn out with feeding a young one, refuse to put the food into the gaping mouth but drop it in the grass instead. "Go ahead. Pick it up. It's time for you to be finding your own food" the old bird seems to be saying.

A focal point for robins each summer in my backyard is a pokeberry plant that has flossy black berries, green berries, and little white flowers all at the same time. It is a really huge plant, fully five feet high, and it continues to produce ripe berries for a long time. The robins have a way of gathering under it late on a fine afternoon, there to sit not far from each other, up to twelve or fifteen at a time, doing absolutely nothing but eating the berries and enjoying the shade. There is no bickering at all. Each bird seems to know that there are berries aplenty. Each keeps itself full, flying up to a fully-laden raceme, yanking off a ripe berry and returning to the ground to swallow it.

I wonder, quite sincerely wonder, about those robins. Are the berries soporific? Are the birds eating more than they should? They are not a very presentable lot, for every one of them, young and old like, is molting; but they are, as a group, the very picture of well-fed contentment.

161

Northern Mockingbird

Mimus polyglottos

The Northern Mockingbird is not brightly colored, but it certainly is among the most noticeable of dooryard birds. It sings loudly from exposed perches, often turning flip-flops while singing. It is intensely combative, sparring fiercely with other mockers that move into its nest territory or—if the season be winter—with birds of any species that take a fancy to a berry supply that it considers its own. Its lively attack on dogs, cats, and human beings that approach its nest too closely is amusing so long as the pecks are received by somebody else. For me, the funniest sight of the neighborhood is a squirrel peacefully making its way along a heavy telephone wire suddenly forced by a mocker to double its speed. The bird actually nips the squirrel and the squirrel feels the nip. Why it doesn't fall from the wire is beyond me. Hotly pursued, and nipped repeatedly, it seeks the protection of a leafy tree just as fast as it can.

The most puzzling activity of the mocker is its wing-flashing. What I'm speaking of is not in any way connected with the flamboyant spreading of wings that accompanies the singing male's flipflops above its favorite chimney, tree-top, or TV aerial. It is largely, almost wholly, terrestrial and it seems to have nothing to do with defense of territory or with courtship. Occasionally, it accompanies the sparring of rival males where territories adjoin. But usually it is a solo performance put on while the individual is quietly searching for food. I see the performance in my backyard almost every day in summer. I'm not sure that I've ever seen it in winter. At times it looks like some sort of calisthenic or sitting-up exercise. It does not always in-

162

Northern Mockingbird, *Mimus polyglottos*. New Mexico, 1958.
Dale A. and Marian A. Zimmerman.

volve a complete spreading of the wings. Sometimes it is a mere lifting or half spreading, but when fully performed the white parts of the fanned-out feathers show very plainly as if intended to startle into flight some grasshopper or other insect. But never—and I say this after years of watching—have I seen a mocker capture an insect that obviously had revealed itself as a result of the flash.

It doesn't sound very scientific to say that the mocker wing-flashes because it can't keep from doing so. But hearken to this: years ago, when I was in uniform and, as officer-of-the-day, was duty-bound to remain at my desk in case an important phone call came through, I watched an almost fledged mocker, well feathered but not yet able to fly, move from under a bush out onto a walk where it was in plain sight. There, obviously hungry, it gave the thin high squeal that baby mockers give to let their parents know where they are. I watched through a window only a

163

few yards away. I could hear the food-calls clearly. What I was not prepared for, indeed what I was shocked by, was that baby bird's full flashing of both its wings high over its head. The flashing did not accompany food visits. I could not for the life of me tell what prompted it. It served no purpose that I could see. Indeed, in my opinion it was worse than useless. It was a mistake, for it could call the attention of a passing shrike, hawk, or cat to an easily obtainable meal. My long-considered guess is that the baby mocker flashed its wings because it had to. The urge to wing-flash was built-in. What is built-in and passed along genetically is inescapable.

Cedar Waxwing

Bombycilla cedrorum

So accustomed are we nowadays to laws protecting birds that it is hard to believe those early ornithologists Elliott Coues and D. Webster Prentiss who, in a 128-page paper published in 1883 on the birdlife of the District of Columbia, said of Cedar Waxwings: "In the fall, when they grow fat, they are frequently offered for sale in the markets." It would be interesting to know what a buyer had to pay per dozen for unplucked Cedar Waxwings or per pound for skinned ones. Thought of such a transaction is a bit appalling, if not disgusting. Bear in mind that in those days no one paid much attention to the economic or aesthetic value of birdlife. People might well have said, "Waxwings are pretty, but there are too many of them. They ruin the cherry crop. If they're good to eat, we might as well eat them!" Waxwings then, as now, went about in big flocks in fall and were easy enough to shoot at that season. The supply must have seemed inexhaustible.

The behavior of Cedar Waxwings in fall and winter leads any thoughtful observer to wonder about such psychic phenomena as the flock-mind. The birds of the flock react so simultaneously to urges or stimuli that they seem not to be several organisms but rather a single fractured one. Closely bunched, they alight in a leafless treetop, content to perch there almost motionless for a quarter of an hour, as if napping. A sudden impulse takes them to the ground, a few at first, then the rest in a steady stream, until all are drinking and bathing at a streetside puddle. So closely massed are they that they hide the water's edge. All seem to be equally thirsty or in need of a bath. Again suddenly, as if every bird has received at the same instant a

165

warning, reminder, or invitation, off they whir, this time to another treetop for a brief period of preening and drying off. They are never very wet, for their sleek plumage seems to shed water. "Now for that old oak with its mistletoe," the flock-mind seems to tell them, so off they go once more, this time for food.

In Oklahoma, Cedar Waxwings eat berries of many sorts—those of mistletoe first, then of hackberry, pyracantha, holly, juniper, mountain ash, and privet in about that order of preference. The mistletoe berries pass through the birds only partly digested, the droppings fall on branches and dry there, rain softens the droppings, the seeds germinate, and lo, there are more mistletoe plants for the waxwings. As for the sweet-tasting hackberries, more information is needed. I know they are swallowed whole, but I don't know which end the big seeds emerge from when the birds eliminate them. In either case, some fall to the ground and germinate there, thus producing more hackberry trees. Scattered junipers that dot open grassland may well have been planted in the same way. As for poison ivy, I have found the berries in flickers' stomachs, but never in the stomach of a Cedar Waxwing.

There is something almost ferocious about the way in which a waxwing flock feeds. The birds do not quarrel or snap at each other, but each goes after berries as if driven, not by hunger but by determination to fill up as promptly as possible. The holly bush, bright red with fruit as the flock alights, is colorful indeed as the birds spread their yellow-tipped tails and flash the white of their under-wings. When they fly off, the red that was there goes with them, for hardly a berry is left.

Toward the end of winter when the berry supply is gone, the waxwings eat buds, young leaves, flowers, and insects. The days become longer and warmer. The waxwing flocks dwindle as pairs form. A very few scattered pairs remain to nest in the southern Great Plains, but most of them move northward. In the summer of 1956 I found

Cedar Waxwing, *Bombycilla cedrorum*. Oklahoma, 1962.
Howard W. Goard.

the species nesting at the mouth of the Moose River at the south end of James Bay.

Cedar Waxwings hatch naked. As the feathers develop, those of the tail emerge from their papillae with tips a shade of light yellow. The nestlings arrange themselves with heads in and tails out—this possibly for sanitary reasons—so the yellow tail-tips make a pretty fringe just above the nest's rim.

Waxwings tend to overeat. A captive that I once had, a young bird rescued from a dog, ate its fill of blueberries, mulberries, or choke cherries whenever we fed it. Always it seemed to want more. At each feeding a limit was reached when the little bird stopped reaching its neck out and settled back with plumage fluffed and eyes half shut. Now the last berry swallowed had a way of slipping from the bill and dropping to the floor. My pet, reacting in a way that was most amusing, fluttered its wings and begged with mouth opened toward the lost berry as if the fervor of entreaty would bring that precious bit back!

Loggerhead Shrike

Lanius ludovicianus

Known widely as the butcherbird and, locally, as the French mockingbird, this predator resembles the mocker in size, in color, and even—to some extent—in song. In behavior, however, it is very different. It never sings boisterously. It never runs about on the lawn, lifting its tail high when stopping to look around. It is rather sedate, given to sitting quietly on a wire or the top of a small tree, looking for prey. It is, as its book name suggests, big-headed. It sits close to its perch, never with legs showing plainly, and holds its tail horizontally.

If obliged to change perches, it drops quickly downward from one, then, a few feet above ground, flies straight across the open field to the other, reaching it with a final swoop upward on widespread wings. Among breeding birds of the southern Great Plains this behavior is unique. Also unique is its impaling of prey on thorns. Thorn-bearing trees of its habitat include the bois d'arc, hawthorn, locust, and mesquite. Barbed wire fences provide "thorns" galore in comparatively treeless areas that are under cultivation or used as cattle range.

I have been puzzled by the loggerhead's butchershops. I sometimes wonder whether what is impaled there is ever used. Sixty years ago R. Crompton Tate found fifty-six grasshoppers and eleven potato beetles on cactus spines near a nest at the west end of the Oklahoma Panhandle, but I have never found such a big larder. So often have I found dried-up lizards and small snakes that I have come to suspect that the shrikes horde prey instinctively when it is abundant and easy to catch, whether they ever use it or not. Putting prey on a thorn no doubt helps with pulling it

Loggerhead Shrike, *Lanius ludovicianus*. New Mexico, 1984.
Dale A. and Marian A. Zimmerman.

to pieces, but shrikes that I have watched never seemed to
have trouble holding a grasshopper with a foot while tearing it apart. Might butchershops be maintained to give
young of the first brood food that they can pull off and eat
while learning to catch prey? Summer butchershops should
be watched on the chance that young of the second brood
may also need help despite the abundance of insects at
that time of year. I have never found freshly impaled prey
in late summer.

Most prey is small, easy to kill, and easy to tear to
pieces, but birds as large as shrikes are sometimes caught,
among them the Northern Cardinal (*Cardinalis cardinalis*), a
big-billed species that could bite the shrike savagely if it
tried. I know of three cardinals that were killed by loggerheads in Oklahoma—a female caught at a feeder in a residential part of Norman; a male (weight 45.0 grams; weight

of shrike, a female, 44.5 grams) caught a few miles east of Norman; and a male caught near Copan, northeastern Oklahoma. Observers who watched the killing of this last one saw the shrike working the carcass into a weed-fork, thus helping it to pull the head off. I doubt that a loggerhead could fly carrying a full-grown cardinal, but I have seen one carrying a Song Sparrow (*Melospiza melodia*) in its bill while flying slowly. Bird prey is killed with a quick bite at the base of the skull. At Stillwater, Oklahoma, where Frederick M. Baumgartner and his wife, Marguerite, ran a banding station for many years, loggerheads were bothersome. One entered a trap in which there were two Harris's Sparrows (*Zonotrichia querula*), killing both of them. I prepared the sparrows as specimens, finding at the base of the skull in each a wound so free of blood that I did not need to wash the plumage.

The loggerhead starts nesting early in the southern Great Plains. A nest holding six eggs was found by Vera Gilmore near Tulsa on March 20, 1927. On March 22, 1959, I observed a pair of birds building a nest in a bois d'arc tree near Norman. Two broods are reared regularly in Oklahoma. Rearing a brood requires about two months, though time is saved if the same nest is used twice.

I have never seen young of the first brood helping their parents with the second brood. Shrikes deserve close study during midsummer when second broods are being reared. Insects may be so abundant at that time of year that there is no need for a butchershop close to the nest.

The loggerhead's song has been described as "creaky and unmusical," but I have not found it so. I recall hearing it for the first time. The day was windy and I could not see the singer, for it was hidden by a hedge. I thought the song was a mocker's—a comment that does not mean much, for a mocker can make many sorts of sounds—but the phrases did not seem to be repeated. The whole performance was pleasing, almost melodious, though it did not sound in the least as if delivered in defense of territory.

Bell's Vireo

Vireo bellii

Smallest of the vireos of the southern Great Plains is the Bell's. It is also usually the easiest to observe. It is not brightly colored, but its two wingbars are conspicuous, and it is almost never hidden among leaves far overhead. In all my years of field work I have never looked straight up at a Bell's Vireo. The sprightly bird lives most of its life below a man's eye level.

The species does not inhabit forests. In parts of the southern Great Plains that I know best, it has been most numerous in sand-plum thickets in open country, in bois d'arc shelter-belts, and in open mesquite woods throughout which the trees are not very large. At Norman, Oklahoma, it was among the commonest birds in the summer of 1955: at least twenty pairs nested in thicketed parts of a 160-acre "wild" tract along the northeast edge of the city. In heavily wooded parts of southeastern Oklahoma it lives in shrubbery along the highways. It is decidedly uncommon west of the 100th meridian. I have seen it once in Texas County, in the Panhandle, but I am not sure that singing male had a mate.

Certainly the most noticeable thing about the Bell's Vireo is its song, a performance that may be described as unmusical, impetuous, polysyllabic, and rushed-through. Only the males sing, and each male sings two different songs, one ending with a rising somewhat interrogatory note, the other with a descending note that sounds like an answer. Whether males always sing the questioning song first when they begin defending a territory I cannot say; but I have listened to hundreds of songs and I have yet to hear a questioning song followed directly by that same song.

Males never sing at the nest as Warbling Vireos (*V. gilvus*) do, but where they sing persistently there is sure to be a nest close by. The nest is a neat cup suspended from a twig in the thicket's very heart or from a low branch between trees in a bois d'arc shelter-belt. It is plain enough to see once found, but finding it may not be easy.

Nests are heavily parasitized by the cowbird. Of twenty-two nests observed by David F. Parmelee in 1954 in central Oklahoma, twelve were parasitized. Of fourteen nests carefully studied in 1955 in south-central Oklahoma by Charles A. Ely, ten were parasitized. Nine of the ten produced no young of either species, and at one the cowbird egg did not hatch and three vireos fledged. Of sixty-one nests studied by Thomas G. Overmire in north-central Oklahoma in 1960 and 1961, eighteen were parasitized, three of which produced three cowbirds each.

When I first gave a course in bird study at the University's Biological Station in 1951, I considered the Bell's Vireo one of the area's commonest birds. It continued to be common in 1954 and 1955, seemed to be less common in 1957 and 1959, and was noticeably uncommon in 1968. Today it is rare in the area, if present at all. Along the road between the station and the village of Willis, two miles away, not a single pair may now be nesting. There have, of course, been habitat changes. Persimmon saplings have grown taller, stands of willow more dense. But sand-plum thickets and bois d'arc shelter-belts have remained about as they were and no land has been drastically cleared.

My feeling that the cowbird's parasitism was proving too much for the vireo in that area came to a climax in 1959. On June 30 of that year, my class and I found a nest containing a large, fit-looking cowbird and four vireo chicks, two small and dead under the cowbird, one small and barely alive partly under the cowbird, and one small but obviously alive, though pale and emaciated, alongside the

Bell's Vireo, *Vireo bellii*. Arkansas, 1983. E. Wayne Easley.

cowbird. I removed the three dead and almost dead chicks that day, leaving the one that looked as if it might survive. The following day the nest held only the cowbird. We could but surmise that the parent vireos had removed and carried off their doomed chick for we could not find it on the ground under the nest.

Some birds, notably the Red-winged Blackbird (*Agelaius phoeniceus*), resent the presence of a female cowbird in their midst. In the spring of 1922, at a big cattail marsh in northwestern Pennsylvania, I saw a company of red-wings drive a female cowbird about until, in desperation, she took refuge in the water among the vegetation close to shore. I caught her and let her go after she dried off (George M. Sutton, 1928, *Ann. Carnegie Mus.* XVIII, p. 163). The point I want to make here is that I have never seen a Bell's Vireo chasing off a cowbird of either sex. The female cowbird evidently finds the vireo's nest, waits close by early in the morning until the vireo leaves, then slips in and lays her egg with or without removing a vireo's egg first.

Warbling Vireo

Vireo gilvus

As a family the vireos are not very brightly colored, and the Warbling Vireo is one of the dullest of the lot. The species' chief field mark is the white line separating the mouse gray of its crown from the olive gray of its ear coverts. The pale yellowish tone of its flanks is more noticeable in the fall after the molt than it is during the breeding season.

Male Warbling Vireos sing full songs, and frequently, in the fall. They also sing at the nest—not near the nest but in it. How much incubating they do I cannot say, but rather than huddling down on the eggs they stand in the nest-cup with tail horizontal over the rim. Their behavior is not in the least secretive. The songs may be in defense of territory, but they sound more like advertisement.

My study of singing males came to a climax in 1946 in southeastern Michigan. That summer I found five nests, one of which (No. 1) was in a big elm close to the laboratory in which I lived. The nest was attached to slender twigs about thirty-five feet up. A Northern Oriole's (*Icterus galbula*) nest was a bit lower on the tree's opposite side. To reach the vireo nest I climbed an extension ladder attached vertically to a truck. At the ladder's top I could steady myself by grasping twigs. The nest was almost finished when I found it on May 26, and a bird was still working on it the following day. It appeared to be finished on May 28, when I first climbed to it. On May 30 it held one egg.

That day the male flew to it shortly after I had descended the ladder. He stood in the nest a few minutes, then began singing full songs. While there, his mate did not join him. On May 31, at 1:05 P.M. I found two eggs in the nest, but saw no bird close by and heard no singing in

Warbling Vireo, *Vireo gilvus*. Michigan, 1967.
Betty Darling Cottrille.

the tree. On June 1, at 7:15 A.M., I saw a bird close by, but heard no singing. At 1:30 P.M. that day I climbed to the nest, finding three eggs. Both birds scolded a little throughout my visit, calling *nyah, nyah*, in a rasping voice. On June 2 a bird was on the nest but it was not singing. I climbed up, finding four eggs. I did not visit the nest on June 3. At 1:00 P.M. on June 4, a bird was on the nest, but it was not singing. One June 5 and 6 I visited the nest-tree twice each day, seeing no bird on the nest and hearing no songs. When I climbed to the nest on June 8, no bird was there, and I heard neither scolding nor singing in the big elm. In the nest was a broken egg, a vireo's, not a cowbird's.

Observations at that nest led me to believe that the female did most, if not all, of the incubating just after completing the clutch. At Nests 4 and 5, found later in the season, incubation might well have been further advanced, for a male sang fervently for considerable stretches of time at each nest. At Nest 4, songs poured down at intervals ranging from ten to twenty seconds at 6:28, 7:30, and 11:15 A.M. I found myself wondering whether the female was doing any incubating at all.

My experience with the Warbling Vireo on the university campus in Norman has been disappointing. In the fall of 1952, I heard both old and young males singing high in big cottonwoods, elms, hackberries, and sycamores day after day. The song of young males were more sputtery than those of adults. Singing males were less common the following spring, but a few pairs continued to nest until 1973. During the 1952–53 period I found three nests on or close to the campus—two in elms, one in a sycamore. At one nest I watched the singing male on several occasions but could not come to any conclusion about whether incubation was well advanced, since I did not even know what the nest contained.

A nest that we did not find probably fledged a brood, for one of my students, John C. Johnson, Jr., found an almost-fledged chick dead on a sidewalk. The little thing was much paler than the adult, especially on the crown.

Often have I wondered about that singing at the nest. Does the boldness of the pronouncement declare the fitness of the singer, convince his mate that all is well, announce that where there is no inhibition there is no cause for alarm? Do the advantages derived from warning other Warbling Vireos to stay on their own territories actually offset the disadvantages of Blue Jay predation? If all this singing at the nest benefits the Warbling Vireo, then why are most bird species so very secretive about their nests?

A suspicion may linger that some songs at nests are actually the songs of female birds. I do not plan to shoot singing birds at nests just to find out.

Northern Cardinal

Cardinalis cardinalis

The Northern Cardinal is a much-loved bird. Its singing is cheerful. It is close by and in evidence throughout the year, for it is strictly non-migratory. Its bright colors enliven the bleakest of winter days. Since my coming to Norman thirty years ago, the species has held its own well. On the university campus several pairs have nested regularly, each pair bringing out two broods every summer that I have been here.

Many people who watch birds closely do not realize that female cardinals sing. Female songs are not quite as long, or quite as ebullient, as male songs, and often they are sung from a hidden position. The observer sees the brilliant male singing from an exposed perch high in a tree. He hears another song not far away and wrongly assumes that a rival male is singing. In my yard I hear both males and females singing every spring about the time nest-building begins. Never do pairs sing a duet, and I have noticed, time after time, that males tend to sing almost *at* me, as if trying to scare me off, while the females stay in the shrubbery, out of sight while singing.

Many cardinals that nest in my neighborhood remain paired all year, and the two birds go about companionably in winter. At that season the male asserts his *macho* superiority by driving the female from the feeding counter until he has eaten his fill. Let spring come round, however, and that same male goes to great lengths cracking sunflower seeds for his mate, giving the tasty kernels to her as if considering her incapable of cracking a seed herself. The delightful part of the scene is the female's coy acceptance of all this attention, quite as if she has forgotten how to use that huge bill of hers.

179

Northern Cardinal, *Cardinalis cardinalis*. Oklahoma, 1983.
John S. Shackford.

Now for some facts about cardinals that may shock some of their human friends. In Oklahoma the cardinal is unquestionably the leading producer of cowbirds. Cowbird egg-laying may not start quite as early as cardinal egg-laying, but first cardinal broods nearly always have at least one cowbird in them and second broods often have two. Many a second brood reared here in Norman is composed wholly of cowbirds, usually two, occasionally three. My notebook is full of August entries pertaining to cardinals observed caring for two cowbirds. Frequent telephone calls inform me of male cardinals followed by "strange-looking" brown birds that walk and that don't look at all like cardinals.

Counting the cowbirds produced by Oklahoma's cardinals would, of course, be impossible. But when we witness the gathering in late summer of huge "blackbird" roosts and realize that literally thousands of cowbirds are in them, we know that the cowbird is abundant indeed.

I can be philosophical about the cowbird's abundance. But when I become aware of the cowbird's widespread elimination of such helpless victims as the Bell's Vireo and realize that the cardinal is responsible for bringing into the world of what may be too many cowbirds for the health of an area's bird population as a whole, I find myself wishing that there were some way of stemming the ugly tide. The cowbirds are interesting. We do not want to exterminate them—quite. But we don't want to lose the Bell's Vireos and the other small birds that disappear as a direct result of the cowbird presence with us.

The cardinal is the cowbird's ideal host. It is only a little larger than a cowbird. Its eggs are so like the cowbird's that even an expert sometimes has trouble telling them apart. It can be argued, I know, that since cowbird and cardinal eggs look much alike, some cowbird eggs will surely be tossed out by the female cowbirds when replacement is going on. But the fact remains that too many late summer cardinal broods are composed of cowbirds. Wouldn't it be interesting if, through long-continued study of banded birds, we should learn that female cowbirds reared by cardinals tended to lay their eggs only in cardinal nests?

The thought crosses my mind that cardinals may have a "soft spot" of some sort in their makeup that gives them a tolerance that most birds do not have. A cardinal that went so far as to feed a goldfish at the edge of a pool has actually been photographed. Down the street in Norman at a house that is surrounded by ornamental trees and shrubbery, a pair of cardinals and a pair of robins have nested year after year. One summer the two nests were only about six feet apart and at least one of the parent robins was observed feeding the nestling cardinals time after time without disturbing the parent cardinals in the least. Karl Maslowski tells me that at Cincinnati, Ohio, a female cardinal and female robin laid their eggs in the same nest (that looked like a robin's) and proceeded to rear both broods quite amicably. The strange performance was fully documented. Imagine those beautiful pale blue robin eggs and the comparatively drab and speckled eggs lying side by side!

Painted Bunting

Passerina ciris

The fully adult male Painted Bunting, with his red under-parts, purplish-blue head, and bright green back is un-believably colorful. He is among the few North American birds that can be called gaudy. No wonder he is known in the southeastern United States as the nonpareil, the unique, the "without equal." The female is dull indeed in comparison. She is olive-green above and light grayish-yellow below. Males in the plumage they wear for a year after molting out of the drab nestling plumage look much like adult females. Such males sing fervently and appear to be defending territories, but I have yet to find one actually fathering a brood. The species is so common in Oklahoma east of the Panhandle that ascertaining vital facts about first-year males should not be difficult.

The Painted Bunting winters in southern Mexico, Central America, and Cuba. Some populations in Florida probably are nonmigratory. Return from the south in spring is announced by singing. Singing males are not shy. They perch on telephone wires and the tops of small trees, but their songs do not "ring out" as those of the Indigo Bunting (*P. cyanea*) do. Singing continues until the first week of August, then abruptly stops. When it stops, the males disappear. No one seems to know where they have gone or what they are doing. This is hardly an overstatement.

Male birds are believed to return in spring ahead of the females, but the females are so inconspicuous in those last days of April that most of them must escape detection. I recall watching what I took to be a female very early one spring and was congratulating myself on being able to publish an arrival date for females when the bird flew to a treetop and started to sing. "She" was a subadult male!

Adult males are so brilliantly colored that no one can be blamed for expecting them to display magnificently when courting. What I have seen of courtship has been disappointing. A display that I observed in southern Oklahoma in 1952 was pretty, though hardly spectacular. The male hung in one spot in the air not far from the female, fluttering his wings and revolving in such a way as to show off first the red of his underparts, then the green of his back. Most displays witnessed by David F. Parmelee during his intensive study of the species in Marshall County, Oklahoma, in 1957 were on the ground. In them the male hopped around the female with head held up and back, occasionally fluttering both wings. One male that he watched flew for thirty yards directly in front of a flying female, flashing the green of his back in display.

The nest is built by the female. It is usually not very far from the ground. Many nests that I have found have been on downward slanting branches of small trees growing along the borders of open pastureland. Nests are often cowbird-parasitized. As a rule, two broods are reared each summer. When the first brood leaves the nest, the male parent takes charge of them while the female proceeds with building another nest. Second nests are usually farther from the ground than first nests. Dr. Parmelee carefully watched the comings and goings of several two-brooded females. One of them, whose new nest was fourteen and a half feet from the old one, "fed a chick, reached out and pulled nesting material from a branch near by, placed the material in her nest several feet away, and flew off to gather more food." All work and no play! According to the Parmelee records, twenty-eight to twenty-nine days pass between the fledging of first and second broods in southern Oklahoma.

What happens to the bright males when they stop singing and disappear? Were it not for an occasional glimpse that we have of one, we might assume that they have left for their winter home. Do they seek a secluded spot and undergo a leisurely postnuptial molt? My belief is that they do not. I have never collected a molting adult male

Painted Bunting, *Passerina ciris*. Florida, 1979. © William E. Ray, Jr./
National Audubon Society Collection, PR.

nor have I found molted feathers in shadowy places where
molt might be going on. I suspect that adult males live
quietly in or near the very territories they defend earlier in
the season; that they move southward in September or
October; and that they molt when they reach their winter home.

But why does the male Painted Bunting not have a dull
winter plumage? What is there about the species that per-
mits the adult males to stay bright all year? Male Indigo
Buntings are dull-colored in winter. The plumage of male
Lazuli and Varied buntings (*P. amoena* and *P. versicolor*) is
edged with brown in winter. Do some male Painted Buntings have brown-edged winter plumage? I have never
handled such a specimen.

Smith's Longspur

Calcarius pictus

When the Sutton family moved into the big house that my father built near the Texas Christian University campus south of Fort Worth, our front yard was the prairie. I was to find many interesting creatures there—jack rabbits, spotted skunks, ground squirrels, race-runner lizards, bull-snakes, and tarantulas among them. In winter the most abundant birds were Western Meadowlarks and McCown's

Smith's Longspur, *Calcarius pictus*. Oklahoma, 1984.
John S. Shackford.

Longspurs (*Calcarius mccownii*). The longspurs went about in huge flocks that had a way of springing up from the grass, of flying around in big circles, of returning to the place from which they had flown, and of forming a layer of fluttering birds a few feet above ground just before alighting. Chestnut-collared Longspurs (*C. ornatus*) were there too, a fact that I confirmed by collecting specimens. As for the Lapland Longspur (*C. lapponicus*) and Smith's Longspur I was in doubt, for I never obtained a specimen of either species in the Fort Worth area.

At Norman, central Oklahoma, only 250 miles north of Fort Worth, we sometimes see longspurs of all four species in winter, but their numbers vary greatly depending, I suppose, on the amount of snowfall, hence of availability of food in the northern Great Plains. At times we have big flocks of laplands or chestnut-collars. The McCown's is here, but the really big flocks of that species that I have seen have been in cattle range and stubble fields just north of the Red River in southwestern Oklahoma.

It is the Smith's, a not-very-well-known bird, that I have seen most regularly near Norman during the 1952–1978 period. I spent much time afield during those winters. I have known just where to find the bird and have had the pleasure of showing it to many a person who had never seen it.

The place to which I usually took visitors from afar was a virtually treeless tract near the airport just northwest of the city. There the dominant grass is a triple-awn of the genus *Aristida*, which forms a thick mat that covers most of the area. Very few weeds grow in this grass, and the Smith's Longspurs feed on the grass's slender seeds.

Not always have we found our birds, but as a rule we would put up a flock as we walked back and forth. The birds did not fly up all at once, but when one or two flushed, the others were presently in the air too, and the little company had a way of flying around and around, quite aimlessly it seemed, and sometimes quite close to us at eye level. All of them, both males and females, had a strong buffy appearance and adult males had noticeably black-and-white lesser wing coverts, a field-mark that was not diagnostic, for male Chestnut-collared Longspurs had it too.

I made the mistake, on one field trip with students, of saying that in winter the Smith's Longspur did not alight anywhere except on the ground. The words were hardly out of my mouth when the whole little flock that we had been watching alighted well apart on a barbed wire fence not far away. All I could say in self-defense was that I had seen males singing from their song-perches in the tops of little spruces, shrubby alders, and low-growing willows on the species' nesting ground at the mouth of the Churchill River on the west coast of Hudson Bay, but that even there the species spent most of its time on the ground.

At Norman we rarely had a good look at the protectively colored birds while they were feeding. I recall having a fine look at one, a beautifully colored adult male, just after a heavy rain. The bird was threading its way rapidly through the wet grass. Obviously disturbed by my close approach, it crouched for several seconds, then resumed working. Confronted by a sizable puddle, it looked up at me, flashed the white of its tail, and fluttered to a spot beyond the puddle. Its behavior was unusual. When put to flight, such a solitary bird usually flew up and away, perhaps to circle widely or to alight in a distant part of the field.

My students and I have collected a fine series of specimens in Oklahoma, not one of which was molting. Each fall I have expected to see a young bird partly in juvenal feather but no such bird has ever shown up. On December 20, 1980, at Tulsa, in northeastern Oklahoma, John S. Tomer and Jerry Sisler saw a male bird that appeared to them to be "in full breeding plumage." This I could hardly believe, for the breeding male is a strikingly colored bird quite unlike the winter bird, especially about the head.

187

Since the bird was not collected, we can but guess that for some reason its postnuptial molt had not taken place.

Our latest spring records for the species are in the first ten days of March. Specimens taken by Joseph A. Grzybowski on March 6, 1979, were not molting. We have no specimen-evidence that molting ever stops or starts in Oklahoma. Birds arrive and depart in winter feather. They do not arrive on their tree-limit breeding ground until the last of May or early June, so they must molt as they move northward—a circumstance that is puzzling, since birds that are migrating should not, it would seem, be "spending" energy at this time on molting.

Red-winged Blackbird

Agelaius phoeniceus

Throughout its wide range the redwing usually nests among cattails, but I have found colonies nesting in low-lying alfalfa fields, among partly inundated buttonbushes and sapling willows and stands of salt cedar well back from the water's edge. Use of several sorts of nesting places is partly responsible for the species' success. The redwing is one of North America's commonest birds.

How common is it? It does not often show up in towns. We have to go to the country to see it. Breeding populations are often large, but it's the winter roosts that are truly impressive. Along the Canadian River's flood plain in cen-

Red-winged Blackbird, *Agelaius phoeniceus*. Florida, 1983.
John H. Kaufmann.

189

tral Oklahoma, there was a huge roost in the winter of 1952–53. The birds flew in from all directions, alighting in dense flocks in trees, then—as darkness gathered—descending to tall, coarse grass in which they slept a few inches above the ground. Many died from various causes at the roost; others were caught by foxes, raccoons, and feral house cats. When my students and I, intent on banding as many as we could catch, ran through the rising hordes after dark with hand-nets, we noticed how much warmer the air was within the roost area than it was elsewhere. A notable feature of the roost was the several big hawks that slept in treetops close by. These did not try to catch the redwings but fed on such carcasses as they could find. I do not know what led to the establishment of that roost. During the following winter it moved to a low-lying area across the river where the birds slept two or three feet above ground in willow and dogwood saplings.

A winter roost at the north end of Lake Overholser in Oklahoma City is so huge that when, at a distance, we see the birds milling about, the flocks resemble smoke. The birds sleep among cattails, and many grackles, starlings, and cowbirds roost with them.

Some redwings in Oklahoma's big roosts are winter visitors from northern parts of the continent. Whether Oklahoma's breeding populations remain here all year is questionable. Some migration southward almost certainly takes place each fall, but the migrants may not go far.

In spring, male redwings arrive well in advance of the females, announce their presence with their *cong-quer-ee* song, and brighten the landscape. As they sing they spread their wings and tail and so lift their feathers as to make the red-and-buff shoulder patches open up like flowers. Females may arrive in dense flocks, some of which pass on to more northerly nesting areas. When the females that "belong" arrive, groups of them settle down with the males and start nesting. The species is strongly polygynous. Each male has from three to five mates.

The females do all the nest-building, but the males defend territories fiercely, warning females of impending dangers and driving off such marauders as crows. When the eggs hatch, the females proceed to find food for the broods. During the first part of the fledging period, males take no food to the young, but about the time the young are ready to leave the nest, males help the females, often bringing food so large that it is difficult for the chicks to swallow.

Among the fledglings there are no cowbirds in Oklahoma, and this fact deserves attention. Cowbirds occasionally lay their eggs in redwing nests, but the female redwings seem to sense that there's something wrong about an egg that is not pale blue scrawled with black, and she pitches the speckled egg out or deserts the nest. I have never seen a female redwing throwing out a cowbird's egg, understand, but I can't help believing that the throwing-out goes on, and regularly. Charles A. Ely, in his study of cowbird parasitism in south-central Oklahoma in 1956, visited several redwing nests daily during the egg-laying period, finding that one nest, obviously ready for eggs, was deserted when a cowbird egg was laid before a redwing egg had been, and another was deserted after one of four redwing eggs had been replaced by a cowbird egg.

Herbert H. Friedmann in his classic work, *The Cowbirds*, calls the redwing "a fairly common but rather local victim" of the cowbird's parasitism. His further comments make clear that at Ithaca, New York, hundreds of nests were found "but never any with cowbirds' eggs," whereas in Nebraska, parasitism was "not an uncommon occurrence." I am convinced that very few cowbirds, if any, are reared in redwing nests in Oklahoma. I have never observed a redwing feeding a cowbird during my residence in the state since 1952. Nor can I ignore the confrontation between redwings and a female cowbird that I witnessed at a big cattail marsh in northwestern Pennsylvania in the spring of 1922 (see page 175).

Common Grackle

Quiscalus quiscula

Crow blackbird and blackbird are other names by which this common bird is known. It is considerably larger than the Red-winged Blackbird and when adult is really handsome with its glossy plumage and snappy, pale yellow eyes. It walks, taking long strides that move its tail off-center with each stride. Thirty years ago it was the only Oklahoma bird with trough-shaped tail, but today the much larger Great-tailed Grackle (*Quiscalus mexicanus*) breeds throughout most of the state, and that species, too, has tail feathers that slant upward on each side, forming a trough that is noticeable especially in males as they fly up from the ground. In both Common and Great-tailed grackles, males are much larger than females.

The Common Grackle is migratory, but not strongly so in the southern part of its range. Males arrive in spring ahead of the females, puff up their plumage as they sing their unmusical songs, and lay claim to territories. Females arrive quietly, eager to begin nesting. The species appears to be polygynous (male mated with two or more females), but I am not sure how many females a given male has. Breeding groups, each composed of two or more males and several females, gather where the species has nested before, and the females, moving about almost as if a single organism rather than several, choose nest-sites and gather material, working with feverish haste until the big, deeply cupped nests are finished. Nesting groups that I have studied in central Oklahoma have been scattered widely in residential areas of towns and most nests have been in the tops of large elms along streets with little traffic.

In the spring of 1971, two males and at least four fe-

192

Common Grackle, *Quiscalus quiscula*. Arkansas, 1984.
E. Wayne Easley.

males summered near my house in Norman, two of the nests being in the same large cedar of Lebanon, but several feet apart. One morning, after I had noticed the grackles' loud scolding, I looked out and up to see a crow hopping along a branch to one of the cedar of Lebanon nests, where it seized an almost fledged nestling and flew off, followed by all the adult grackles of the neighborhood, an irate mob.

Nests are not always in trees. In Pittsburgh, Pennsylvania, in the summer of 1921, a colony nested among vines covering an old building. At the west end of the Oklahoma Panhandle, a colony has nested for many years in the iron-work on the underside of a bridge. Near Guymon, Oklahoma, on May 16, 1955, I found a small colony nesting with redwings among cattails. Occasionally nests are in cavities in trees. One such nest that I found on May 27, 1971, was eight feet up in a dead tree along the Cimarron River several miles downstream from the bridge mentioned above. While I was examining the nest, two male and several female grackles scolded me. I looked briefly for other nests, but found none.

The species is usually one-brooded, but that it reproduces itself successfully is evident enough when old and young birds assemble at roosts. Roosts in town are a nuisance. Every summer since I have lived on West Brooks Street in Norman, my neighbors and I have had a "blackbird problem." Thickly-leaved old hackberry trees on our side of the street have—to the annoyance of all who use the sidewalk—been just what the grackles liked, for hundreds of them have slept there from about the first week of July on for several weeks. In trying to break up the roost we have pounded on garbage cans, dropped on the walk a fiber tray that clattered loudly, clapped our hands, etc. One year the police joined me in blazing away with shotguns; another year they gave me firecrackers to throw at the birds and a neighbor hung rubber snakes among high branches—all to no avail. After watching the hordes as they gathered, evening after evening, I decided that where several birds settled down, they make a contented noise that told other grackles of the good spot they had found. If only, I thought to myself, we could keep those birds from sounding so contented!

In the summer of 1981, the roost started during the last week of June. At first most of the birds were adult males. Then adult females and young birds began to show up, along with molted feathers among the sidewalk droppings. The tail-shape of incoming birds showed that most of them, adults and young alike, were molting.

The roost broke up in September. I do not know what caused the birds to leave. I believe it was something aside from the din that my neighbors and I had raised. I would not have known how completely they had gone had I not, while being driven along the southwest edge of town on the evening of September 17, seen a steady stream of grackles flying to a roosting spot in the country.

Brown-headed Cowbird

Molothrus ater

As a youngster my feelings about cowbirds were not mixed. They bordered on hatred. How could cowbirds expect anything but hatred when they had such reprehensible habits? My feelings may have been traceable to what I read in Frank M. Chapman's *Bird-Life*, the only bird book I had. Chapman called the cowbird "a thoroughly contemptible creature, lacking in every moral and maternal instinct." The bird fully deserved the hatred I felt. It should, if possible, be exterminated. When I found a cowbird's egg in the nest of some defenseless smaller species, I hurled it to the ground, convinced that the harder I hurled, the more the species "cowbird" would suffer.

Then I began noticing that no nest of robin, Brown Thrasher (*Toxostoma rufum*) or Gray Catbird (*Dumetella carolinensis*) ever held a cowbird egg, while vireo and warbler nests usually held one cowbird egg or more in addition to those of the "host." I decided to leave some cowbird eggs in nests to see what happened. The more closely I watched, the more interested I became. Presently, I was to learn that a cowbird egg was often a replacement, for I found the remains of a pitched-out egg on the ground under the nest, and the pitched-out egg was that of the host. Occasionally I found a nest holding nothing but cowbird eggs. My research reached a climax in West Virginia in 1919 when I found an almost finished Scarlet Tanager (*Piranga olivacea*) nest with a cowbird egg buried in its lining. When I next climbed to the nest, it held three tanager eggs and one cowbird egg. When, a day or so later, I collected the nest, it held *three* cowbird eggs and two tanager eggs plus the cowbird egg in the lining.

Today I no longer hate the cowbird. I watch it with great interest, realizing that—along with the rest of us—it is living its days out with what the inexorable process of evolution has given it. Female cowbirds lay eggs, but they have no inner urge, no instinct, to incubate them, to build a nest, or to care for a brood. Male cowbirds take very seriously their part in the reproductive process, for they go through elaborate displays that look as if designed to intimidate rather than attract. The statement may sound flippant, but when spring returns, watch carefully those little companies of cowbirds that fly past. Some are composed of one female and several males. But some are of males only and there is nothing more outlandish than the sudden wing-spreading, deep bowing, and squeaky singing of a male cowbird displaying in front of the other males. The urge to display must be very strong. Sometimes it overtakes a male while he is on the ground. Now, before his display is over, he has literally fallen forward on his face.

So the cowbird exists because "host species" tolerate its eggs despite the fact that these sometimes differ strikingly in color or size from their own. A Dickcissel's (*Spiza americana*) eggs are a fine light blue. A cowbird's egg among them is noticeably different, but the female Dickcissel—the female does all the incubating—does not seem to care. The strangest thing about the whole business is that the host species seems just as eager to find food for the impostor as for its own young.

How did this social parasitism come to pass? Was the ancestral cowbird orthodox in its nesting? Did the laying of eggs in other nests than one's own start with the discovery by one lazy female cowbird that she could lay her eggs in another cowbird's nest and get away with it? Was it an easy step from laying eggs in another cowbird's nest to laying eggs in the nests of birds that were not cowbirds and thus, gradually, finding that there was no point in building a nest of one's own? Female cowbirds that had this laziness must somehow have been the individuals that survived

Brown-headed Cowbird, *Molothrus ater*. Texas, 1962.
Dale A. and Marian A. Zimmerman.

longest or reproduced most successfully, for as the eons
passed the cowbird became what it is today. What I have
said seems to place the blame on the female element of the
population. Bear in mind that I am not blaming anyone. I
am merely trying to figure out how the phenomenon has
come to be.

Earlier this summer after I had been trimming the
edges of flower beds in my backyard, I sat on a step for
a rest. The day was hot, but the air was stirring and I
enjoyed the shade. While I sat there, a female cowbird
flew past, alighted in the recently mowed grass a rod or
so away, stood high as she looked about, then to my surprise walked slowly—in that delicate way cowbirds have—
straight toward me. When about twelve feet away (I mea-
sured the distance), she sank to her belly, half-closed her
eyes, and also rested. Never, before or since, have I so enjoyed the company of a cowbird.

American Goldfinch

Carduelis tristis

Puzzling is the fact that the American Goldfinch is uncommon in Oklahoma in summer. The few that are here at that season probably are breeding, but very few nests have been found and all of these have been in the northern half of the state. Adult birds that I saw occasionally in south-central Oklahoma in 1954 may have been nesting, but I found no nests that summer. A pair that I observed in Murray County on July 20 were accompanied by dull-plumaged birds that I considered their progeny, but the date was early for fledging, and what I thought were young birds could have been molting adults.

The species is abundant throughout Oklahoma in winter, especially in unforested areas where thistle, wild sunflower, and other weeds that produce great quantities of seeds are common. It obviously is built for comfortable existence in cold-weather areas, for the papillae of its skin produce a thousand more feathers in winter than in summer. Its coming to Oklahoma in winter is not migration of the usual sort; it is, rather, a moving about in search of a dependable food supply above snow. The species' refusal to nest in spring, along with most other birds, may be traceable to the same instinct for keeping comfortable, whatever the season. Successful brood-rearing requires a good supply of newly-formed seeds, so courtship and establishment of nest territories are delayed until midsummer, when a fresh crop of protein-rich seeds is available. There certainly is no midsummer shortage of newly-formed seeds in Oklahoma, so we are obliged to look further for an explanation of the species' rarity here as a breeding bird.

On the basis of what has been observed thus far, I suspect that egg-laying never starts in Oklahoma before the last week in May: on June 1, 1927, at Tulsa, Vera Gilmore found a nest with three eggs, at least two of which had been laid in May. Nest-building has been observed as late as August 27 (Washington County, northeastern Oklahoma). Lateness of nest-building can, of course, result from destruction of early nests; but then, to our surprise, we find young in nests as late as September 17 (Woodward County, northwestern Oklahoma) and September 25 (Cleveland County, central Oklahoma), so we know that late breeding can produce progeny. I have no proof that late broods in Oklahoma are second broods for the season.

Nests are strong-walled cups so tightly built that they hold water in which the chicks sometimes drown. Both parents feed the young and feeding is by regurgitation. Parents do not carry off the fecal sacs, so these accumulate in an almost decorative mass on the outside of the nest wall.

Fledglings leave the nest well feathered in a dull plumage that looks much like the winter plumage of the adult. Is it conceivable that this dull plumage is not lost through molt but held as a true winter plumage with a thousand more feathers than a summer plumage? So far as I know, the feathers of a just-fledged young bird have never been counted. August and September in Oklahoma can be very hot. A young goldfinch wearing many more feathers than it needs might, it would seem, die from the heat. Here may be the explanation we are searching for: if many fledglings die when the weather is excessively hot, reproduction in Oklahoma is not successful.

Where the American Goldfinch is common in summer, it sometimes nests almost colonially. In southeastern Michigan in 1949, I found several pairs breeding not far from each other, each with nest in a separate tree, but all so close to an abundant food supply that there was an almost constant movement of adult birds from nests to seeds throughout the entire breeding season. The brilliant sing-

199

American Goldfinch, *Carduelis tristis*. Arkansas, 1983.
E. Wayne Easley.

ing of the males as they flew in wide circles of figure eights above the nests was delightful to witness. Females on nests often responded to the singing with a sweet, slightly plaintive *dee-dee* or *bay-bee*.

The cowbird parasitizes the American Goldfinch throughout much of the latter's range, this despite the fact that much goldfinch egg-laying continues after that of the cowbird has stopped. But what happens in Oklahoma? A nest found by Margaret M. Nice on July 22, 1920, at Norman, held two goldfinch eggs and two cowbird eggs. The nest was "4 feet from ground in mulberry"—considerably lower than any nest I have found. We have no information as to what happened at that nest. No other Oklahoma goldfinch nest of the thirteen so far reported was parasitized.

House Sparrow

Passer domesticus

While in uniform in World War II, I sometimes felt that I had deserted birds and bird study altogether. A memorable letter that I received during that stressful period was from Alexander Wetmore, Secretary of the Smithsonian Institution at the time and one of America's truly great ornithologists. I can't quote from his letter verbatim, but some of it went like this: "When I begin to feel that I've lost touch with birds, I swing my chair around so I can look out the window and watch the sparrows. They're always interesting."

Often called the English Sparrow because it came to the

House Sparrow, *Passer domesticus*. New York, 1981. © Sidney Bahrt/ National Audubon Society Collection, PR.

201

United States from England through a series of importations dating back to 1850, the House Sparrow now breeds virtually the continent over—south of the polar region. At Churchill, Manitoba, in the summer of 1931, I was surprised to find a population of the hardy birds living about the roundhouse at the northern terminus of the famed Hudson Bay Railroad. I was not sure that they were breeding. They did not stray far from the big building, for Merlins nesting in the spruce woods close by were on the lookout for them. The sparrows had made their way to this subarctic outpost on freight cars carrying grain that would be sent to Liverpool in ships. I have been told that Churchill is not much of a town today, but I venture the guess that the House Sparrows are still there . . . and flourishing.

Passer domesticus is nonmigratory, so it can be studied at any time of year. It has a long breeding season and may rear two or three broods each summer. In England it is said to rear three. Whether females hatched at Temperate Zone latitudes ever start breeding before they are a year old I cannot say, but the impression created by an average House Sparrow population is that breeding is going on much of the time. Only a few days ago, on September 13, 1981, someone found a broken small bird's egg on the hood of his car. I knew from a description of it that it was a freshly laid sparrow's egg.

Male House Sparrows display before females in really cold weather if the day is sunny and the spot is out of the wind. Now, showing off, they fluff up, let their wings droop, lift their tails, and hop around, chirping loudly. If spring has indeed arrived, they go a big step further. Finding a feather, they strut around carrying it as if in hopes that females will "get the idea" and start building nests. I have never seen a female sparrow carrying a feather around in this way.

In the heart of Pittsburgh one fine spring day, I saw a male sparrow hopping about on a curbstone with the small end of an ice cream cone in his bill. He probably was showing off before some female, but he reminded me of a self-righteous person soliciting funds for some worthy cause.

Males sometimes gang up on a female in a way that can be amusing to an observer. They chatter incessantly as they "boil" around the silent female, for all the world as if bent on overwhelming her by sheer force of noise or numbers. During these set-tos—for which British ornithologists doubtless have a charming word—the males are so close together that they can hardly be counted and they move through the shrubbery in an amoeboid mass, stepping on and tumbling over one another, each trying, I suppose, to get as close to the female as possible, perhaps intent on raping her. Suddenly off she flies, and the gang either follows closely and resumes the set-to when she alights, or scatters in all directions as if there'd been no point to any of it. Why the fussing comes to an end I do not know. Perhaps by observing more closely I'll learn what happens. Besieged females are obviously annoyed. They sometimes bite the males savagely, though I've never witnessed a pulling out of feathers.

House Sparrows work hard at nest-building. The nest is a great ball of dry grass with entrance at the side and with a lining of feathers. Nests are often built in martin houses and in Cliff and Barn swallow nests in culverts. Barn Swallow nests are usually so close to the ceiling that there's hardly room for the sparrow nests. Throughout the Panhandle, sparrow nests are often placed well above-ground in trees along the highways. A nest in Texas County was among the coarse foundational twigs of an old White-necked Raven's nest.

Flocks of the Panhandle's sparrows spend much of their time, even in winter, in the dead tumbleweed that gathers in dense masses along fences. I wonder if they eat the tumbleweed seeds. I suspect that they are sometimes caught by shrikes, but I have yet to find a House Sparrow impaled on a wire-barb or thorn anywhere in Oklahoma.

Index of Common Names

Index of Scientific Names

Birds Worth Watching,
designed by Bill Cason,
was set in Palatino by G&S Typesetters
and printed and bound by Dai Nippon.